PRACTICAL PACKET ANALYSIS

PRACTICAL PACKET ANALYSIS

Using Wireshark to Solve Real-World Network Problems

by Chris Sanders

NO STARCH
PRESS

San Francisco

PRACTICAL PACKET ANALYSIS. Copyright © 2007 by Chris Sanders.

 Printed on recycled paper in the United States of America

11 10 09 08 07   1 2 3 4 5 6 7 8 9

ISBN-10: 1-59327-149-2
ISBN-13: 978-1-59327-149-7

Publisher: William Pollock
Production Editor: Christina Samuell
Cover and Interior Design: Octopod Studios
Developmental Editor: William Pollock
Technical Reviewer: Gerald Combs
Copyeditor: Megan Dunchak
Compositor: Riley Hoffman
Proofreader: Elizabeth Campbell
Indexer: Nancy Guenther

For information on book distributors or translations, please contact No Starch Press, Inc. directly:

No Starch Press, Inc.
555 De Haro Street, Suite 250, San Francisco, CA 94107
phone: 415.863.9900; fax: 415.863.9950; info@nostarch.com; www.nostarch.com

Library of Congress Cataloging-in-Publication Data

Sanders, Chris, 1986-
  Practical packet analysis : using Wireshark to solve real-world network problems / Chris Sanders.
      p. cm.
  ISBN-13: 978-1-59327-149-7
  ISBN-10: 1-59327-149-2
 1. Computer network protocols. 2. Packet switching (Data transmission) I. Title.
TK5105.55.S265 2007
004.6'6--dc22

                                      2007013453

I would like to dedicate *Practical Packet Analysis* to my loving parents and my loving God. It is through their combined efforts that all of my success is possible.

> "Trust in the LORD with all thine heart; and lean not unto thine own understanding. In all thy ways acknowledge him, and he shall direct thy paths."
>
> *Proverbs 3:5–6*

BRIEF CONTENTS

CONTENTS IN DETAIL

3
INTRODUCTION TO WIRESHARK 27

4
WORKING WITH CAPTURED PACKETS 39

5
ADVANCED WIRESHARK FEATURES 51

6
COMMON PROTOCOLS   61

7
BASIC CASE SCENARIOS   77

8
FIGHTING A SLOW NETWORK

99

9
SECURITY-BASED ANALYSIS 121

10
SNIFFING INTO THIN AIR 135

11
FURTHER READING

AFTERWORD

INDEX

ACKNOWLEDGMENTS

First and foremost, I would like to thank God for giving me the strength and fortitude it took to complete this project. When my to-do list grew longer and longer and there was no end in sight, he was the one who helped me through all of the stressful times.

I want to thank Bill, Tyler, Christina, and the rest of the team at No Starch Press for giving me the opportunity to write this book and allowing me the creative freedom to do it my way. I would also like to thank Gerald Combs for having the drive and motivation to maintain the Wireshark program, as well as perform the technical edit of this book. Special thanks go out to Laura Chappell, as well, for providing some of the best packet analysis training materials you will find, including several of the packet captures used here.

Personally speaking, I would like to thank Tina Nance, Eddy Wright, and Paul Fletcher for helping me along the path that has led me to this high point in my career. You guys have been great spiritual and professional mentors as well as great friends. Along with that, I have several amazing friends who managed to put up with me while I was writing this book, which is an accomplishment in itself. I would like to extend a very special thank you to Mandy, Barry, Beth, Chad, Jeff, Sarah, and Brandon. I couldn't have done it without you guys behind me.

Mostly, however, I want to thank my loving parents, Kenneth and Judy Sanders. Dad, even though you have never laid hands on a computer, your constant support and nurturing is the reason all of this was possible. Nothing makes me more driven than the desire to hear you say that you are proud of me. Mom, you have been gone from us for five years as of the writing of this book, and although you couldn't be around to see this achievement, you are always in my heart, and that is my true driving force. The passion you showed for living life is what has inspired me to be so passionate in what I do. This book is every bit as much your accomplishment as it is mine.

INTRODUCTION

I got my first computer when I was nine years old. As things go with technology, it broke within about a year. It was enough of a stretch for my family to afford a computer in the first place, and paying for it to be fixed was just financially impossible. However, after a little reading and experimentation, I fixed the computer myself, and that's where my interest in technology began.

That interest evolved into a passion through high school and college, and as that passion grew, so did my abilities, naturally leading me to situations in which I really needed to dig further into network and computer problems. This is when I stumbled upon the Wireshark project (it was called *Ethereal* at the time). This software allowed me to enter a completely new world. Being able to analyze problems in new ways and having the ability to see raw protocols on the wire gave me limitless power in computer and network troubleshooting.

The great thing about packet analysis is that it has become an increasingly popular method of solving problems and learning more about networks. Thanks to the advent of user groups, wikis, and blogs, the techniques covered in this book are becoming prerequisite knowledge for some jobs. Packet analysis is a requirement for managing today's networks, and this book will give you the jump start you need in learning how it all works.

Why This Book?

You may find yourself wondering why you should buy this book as opposed to any other book about packet analysis. The answer lies right in the title: *Practical Packet Analysis*. Let's face it—nothing beats real-world experience, and the closest you can come to that experience in a book is through practical examples of packet analysis with real-world case scenarios. The first half of this book gives you the prerequisite knowledge you will need to understand packet analysis and Wireshark. The second half of the book is devoted entirely to practical case scenarios that you could easily encounter in day-to-day network management.

Whether you are a network technician, a network administrator, a chief information officer, a desktop technician, or simply a help desk worker, you have a lot to gain from understanding and using packet analysis techniques.

Concepts and Approach

I am generally a really laid-back guy, so I when I teach a concept, I try to do so in a really laid-back way. This holds true for the language used in this book. It is very easy to get lost in technical jargon when dealing with a technical concept, but I have tried my best to keep things as casual as possible. I'll make all definitions clear, straightforward, and to the point, without any added fluff.

If you really want to learn packet analysis, you should make it a point to master the concepts in the first several chapters—they are integral to understanding the rest of the book. The second half of the book is purely conceptual. You may not see these exact scenarios in your work, but you should be able to apply the concepts you learn from them in the situations you do encounter.

Here is a quick breakdown of the chapters of this book.

Chapter 1: Packet Analysis and Network Basics

What is packet analysis? How does it work? How do you do it? This chapter covers the very basics of network communication and packet analysis.

Chapter 2: Tapping into the Wire

This chapter covers the different techniques you can use to place a packet sniffer on your network.

Chapter 3: Introduction to Wireshark

Here we'll look at the basics of Wireshark—where to get it, how to use it, what it does, why it's great, and all of that good stuff.

Chapter 4: Working with Captured Packets

Once you get Wireshark up and running, you will want to know the basics of interacting with captured packets. This is where you'll learn.

Chapter 5: Advanced Wireshark Features

Once you have learned to crawl, it's time to take off running with the advanced Wireshark features. This chapter delves into these features and goes under the hood to show you things that aren't always so apparent.

Chapter 6: Common Protocols

This chapter shows what some of the most common network communication protocols look like at the packet level. In order to understand how these protocols can malfunction, you first have to understand how they work.

Chapter 7: Basic Case Scenarios

This chapter contains the first set of real-world case scenarios. Each scenario is presented in an easy-to-follow format, where for each scenario the problem, my analysis, and a solution are given. These basic scenarios deal with only a few computers and involve a limited amount of analysis—just enough to get your feet wet.

Chapter 8: Fighting a Slow Network

The most common problems network technicians hear about generally involve slow network performance. This chapter is devoted to solving these types of problems.

Chapter 9: Security-based Analysis

Network security is the biggest hot button topic in network administration. Because of this, Chapter 9 shows you the ins and outs of solving security-related issues with packet analysis techniques.

Chapter 10: Sniffing into Thin Air

The last chapter of the practical section of the book is a primer on wireless packet analysis. This chapter discusses the differences between wireless analysis and wired analysis and includes a quick case scenario that reinforces what you've learned.

Chapter 11: Further Reading

The final chapter of the book sums up what you have learned and includes some other reference tools and websites you might find useful as you continue to use the packet analysis techniques you have learned.

How to Use This Book

I have intended this book to be used in two ways. The first is, of course, as an educational text that you will read through, chapter by chapter, in order to gain an understanding of packet analysis. This means paying particular attention to the real-world scenarios in the last several chapters. The other use of this book is as a reference resource. There are some features of Wireshark that you will not use very often, so you may forget how they work. Because of this, *Practical Packet Analysis* is a great book to have on your bookshelf should you need a quick refresher about how to use a specific feature.

About the Example Capture Files

All of the capture files used in this book are available at http://www.nostarch .com/packet.htm. In order to maximize the potential of this book, I would highly recommend you download these files and use them as you follow along with the book.

Several of these capture files were contributed by Laura Chappell of the Packet Analysis Institute and Wireshark University. Those captures are as follows:

- blaster.pcap
- destunreachable.pcap
- dosattack.pcap
- double-vision.pcap
- email-troubles.pcap
- evilprogram.pcap
- ftp-crack.pcap
- ftp-uploadfailed.pcap
- gnutella.pcap
- hauntedbrowser.pcap
- http-client-refuse.pcap
- http-fault-post.pcap
- icmp-tracert-slow.pcap
- osfingerprinting.pcap
- slowdownload.pcap
- tcp-con-lost.pcap

1

PACKET ANALYSIS AND NETWORK BASICS

A million different things can go wrong with a computer network on any given day—from a simple spyware infection to a complex router configuration error—and it is impossible to solve every problem immediately. The best we can hope to do is be fully prepared with the knowledge and the tools it takes to respond to these types of issues. All network problems stem from the packet level, where even the prettiest-looking applications can reveal their horrible implementations and seemingly trustworthy protocols can prove malicious. To better understand and solve network problems, we go to the packet level where nothing is hidden from us, where nothing is obscured by misleading menu structures, eye-catching graphics, or untrustworthy employees. Here there are no secrets, and the more we can do at the packet level, the more we can control our network and solve problems. This is the world of packet analysis.

This book dives into the world of packet analysis headfirst. You'll learn what packet analysis is before we delve into network communication, so you can gain some of the basic background you'll need to examine different scenarios. You'll learn how to use the features of the Wireshark packet analysis tool to tackle slow network communication, identify application bottlenecks, and even track hackers through some real-world scenarios. By the time you have finished reading this book, you should be able to implement advanced packet analysis techniques that will help you solve even the most difficult problems in your own network.

What Is Packet Analysis?

Packet analysis, often referred to as *packet sniffing* or *protocol analysis*, describes the process of capturing and interpreting live data as it flows across a network in order to better understand what is happening on that network. Packet analysis is typically performed by a *packet sniffer*, a tool used to capture raw network data going across the wire. Packet analysis can help us understand network characteristics, learn who is on a network, determine who or what is utilizing available bandwidth, identify peak network usage times, identify possible attacks or malicious activity, and find unsecured and bloated applications.

There are various types of packet sniffing programs, including both free and commercial ones. Each program is designed with different goals in mind. A few of the more popular packet analysis programs are tcpdump (a command-line program), OmniPeek, and Wireshark (both GUI-based sniffers).

Evaluating a Packet Sniffer

There are several types of packet sniffers. When selecting the one you're going to use, you should consider the following variables:

- Supported protocols
- User friendliness
- Cost
- Program support
- Operating system support

Supported Protocols

All packet sniffers can interpret various protocols. Most sniffers can interpret all of the most common protocols such as DHCP, IP, and ARP, but not all can interpret some of the more nontraditional protocols. When choosing a sniffer, make sure that it supports the protocols you're going to use.

User Friendliness

Consider the packet sniffer's program layout, ease of installation, and general flow of standard operations. The program you choose should fit your level of expertise. If you have very little packet analysis experience, you may want to avoid the more advanced command-line packet sniffers like tcpdump. On the contrary, if you have a wealth of experience, you may find a more advanced program to be a better choice.

Cost

The great thing about packet sniffers is that there are lots of free ones that rival any commercial product. You should never have to pay for a packet sniffing application.

Program Support

Even once you have mastered the basics of a sniffing program, you will probably still need occasional support to solve new problems as they arise. When evaluating available support, look for things such as developer documentation, public forums, and mailing lists. Although there may be a lack of developer support for free packet sniffing programs like Wireshark, the communities that use these applications will often make up for this. These communities of users and contributors provide discussion boards, wikis, and blogs designed to help you to get more out of your packet sniffer

Operating System Support

Unfortunately, not all packet sniffers support every operating system. Make sure that the one you choose to learn will work on all the operating systems that you need to support.

How Packet Sniffers Work

The packet sniffing process can be broken down into three steps: collection, conversion, and analysis.

Collection

In the first step, the packet sniffer switches the selected network interface into *promiscuous mode*. In this mode the network card can listen for all network traffic on its particular network segment. The sniffer uses this mode along with low-level access to the interface to capture the raw binary data from the wire.

Conversion

In this step, the captured binary data is converted into a readable form. This is where most advanced command-line–driven packet sniffers stop. At this point, the network data is in a form that can be interpreted only on a very basic level, leaving the majority of the analysis to the end user.

Analysis

The third and final step involves the actual analysis of the captured and converted data. In this step the packet sniffer takes the captured network data, verifies its protocol based on the information extracted, and begins its analysis of that protocol's specific features.

Further analysis is performed by comparing multiple packets as well as various other network elements.

How Computers Communicate

In order to fully understand packet analysis, you need to understand exactly how computers communicate with each other. In this section we'll examine the basics of network protocols, the OSI model, network data frames, and the hardware that supports it all.

Networking Protocols

Modern networks are made up of a variety of different systems running on many different platforms. To aid this communication, we use a set of common languages called *network protocols* that govern network communication. Common network protocols include TCP, IP, ARP, and DHCP. A *protocol stack* is a logical grouping of protocols that work together.

A network protocol can be extremely simple or highly complex, depending on its function. Although the various network protocols are often drastically different, most have to address the following issues:

Flow control The generation of messages by the receiving system that instruct the sending system to speed up or slow down its transmission of data

Packet acknowledgment The transmission of a return message from the receiving system to the sending system to acknowledge the receipt of data

Error detection The use of codes by the sending system to verify that the data sent wasn't damaged during transmission

Error correction The retransmission of data that was lost or damaged during the initial transmission

Segmentation The division of long streams of data into smaller ones for more efficient transfer

Data encryption A function that uses cryptographic keys to protect data transmitted across a network

Data compression A method for reducing the size of data transmitted across a network by eliminating redundant information

The Seven-Layer OSI Model

Protocols are separated based on their functions using an industry-standard reference model called the *Open Systems Interconnections (OSI) reference model.* This model was originally published in 1983 by the International Organization for Standardization (ISO) as a document called ISO 7498.

The OSI model divides the network communications process into seven distinct layers:

- Application (Layer 7)
- Presentation (Layer 6)
- Session (Layer 5)
- Transport (Layer 4)

- Network (Layer 3)
- Data link (Layer 2)
- Physical (Layer 1)

The seven layers in the hierarchical OSI model (Figure 1-1) make it much easier to understand network communication. The application layer at the top represents the actual programs used to access network resources. The bottom layer is the physical layer, through which the actual network data travels. The protocols at each layer work together to package data for the next layer up.

NOTE *The OSI model is no more than an industry-recommended standard; protocol developers are not required to follow it exactly. As a matter of fact, the OSI model is not the only networking model that exists—for example, some people prefer the Department of Defense (DoD) model. We'll work around the concepts of the OSI model in this book, so we won't cover the DoD model here.*

Let's take a broad look at the functions of each of the OSI model's layers as well as some examples of the protocols used in each.

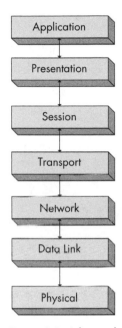

Figure 1-1: A hierarchical view of the seven layers of the OSI model

The Application Layer

The *application layer*, the topmost layer on the OSI model, provides a means for users to actually access network resources. This is the only layer typically seen by end users, as it provides the interface that is the base for all of their network activities.

The Presentation Layer

The *presentation layer* transforms the data it receives into a format that can be read by the application layer. The data encoding and decoding done here depends on the application layer protocol that is sending or receiving the data. This layer also handles several forms of encryption and decryption used for securing data.

The Session Layer

The *session layer* manages the *dialog*, or session between two computers; it establishes, manages, and terminates this connection among all communicating devices. The session layer is also responsible for establishing whether a connection is duplex or half-duplex and for gracefully closing a connection between hosts, rather than dropping it abruptly.

The Transport Layer

The primary purpose of the *transport layer* is to provide reliable data transport services to lower layers. Through features including flow control, segmentation and desegmentation, and error control, the transport layer makes sure data gets from point to point error free. Because ensuring reliable data transportation can be extremely cumbersome, the OSI model devotes an entire layer to it. The transport layer provides its services to both connection-oriented and connectionless protocols. Firewalls and proxy servers operate at this layer.

The Network Layer

The *network layer* is responsible for routing data between physical networks, and it is one of the most complex OSI layers. It is responsible for the logical addressing of network hosts (for example, through an IP address), and it also handles packet segmentation, protocol identification, and in some cases, error detection. Routers operate at this layer.

The Data Link Layer

The *data link layer* provides a means of transporting data across a physical network. Its primary purpose is to provide an addressing scheme that can be used to identify physical devices and provide error-checking features to ensure data integrity. Bridges and switches are physical devices that operate at this layer.

The Physical Layer

The *physical layer* at the bottom of the OSI model is the physical medium through which network data is transferred. This layer defines the physical and electrical nature of all hardware used, including voltages, hubs, network adapters, repeaters, and cabling specifications. The physical layer establishes and terminates connections, provides a means of sharing communication resources, and converts signals from digital to analog and vice versa.

Table 1-1 lists some of the more common protocols used at each individual layer of the OSI model.

Table 1-1: Typical Protocols Used in Each Layer of the OSI Model

Layer	Protocol
Application	HTTP, SMTP, FTP, Telnet
Presentation	ASCII, MPEG, JPEG, MIDI
Session	NetBIOS, SAP, SDP, NWLink
Transport	TCP, UDP, SPX
Network	IP, ICMP, ARP, RIP, IPX
Data Link	Ethernet, Token Ring, FDDI, AppleTalk

Protocol Interaction

How does data flow up and down through the OSI model? The initial data transfer on a network begins at the application layer of the transmitting system. Data works its way down the seven layers of the OSI model until it reaches the physical layer, at which point the physical layer of the transmitting system sends the data to the receiving system. The receiving system picks up the data at its physical layer, and the data proceeds up the remaining layers of the receiving system to the application layer at the top.

Services provided by various protocols at any given level of the OSI model are not redundant. For example, if a protocol at one layer provides a particular service, then no other protocol at any other layer will provide this same service. Protocols at corresponding layers on the sending and receiving computers are complementary. If a protocol on layer seven of the sending computer is responsible for encrypting the data being transmitted, then the corresponding protocol on layer seven of the receiving machine is expected to be responsible for decrypting that data. Figure 1-2 shows a graphical representation of the OSI model as it relates to two communicating clients. Here you can see communication going from top to bottom on one client and then reversing when it reaches the second client.

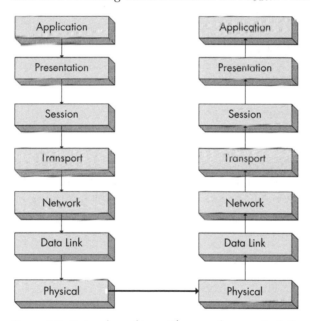

Figure 1-2: Protocols working at the same layer on both the sending and receiving systems

Each layer in the OSI model is only capable of communicating with the layers directly above and below it. For example, layer two can only send and receive data from layers one and three.

Data Encapsulation

The protocols on different layers communicate with the aid of *data encapsulation*. Each layer in the stack is responsible for adding a header or footer to the data being communicated, and these extra bits of information allow the layers to communicate. For example, when the transport layer receives data from the session layer, it adds its own header information to that data before passing it to the next layer.

The Protocol Data Unit

The encapsulation process creates a *protocol data unit (PDU)*, which includes the data being sent and all header or footer information added to it.

As data moves down the OSI model, the PDU changes and grows as header and footer information from various protocols is added to it. The PDU is in its final form once it reaches the physical layer, at which point it is sent to the destination computer. The receiving computer strips the protocol headers and footers from the PDU as the data climbs up the OSI layers. Once the PDU reaches the top layer of the OSI model, only the original data remains.

NOTE *The term* packet *is associated with the term* Protocol Data Unit (PDU). *When I use the word* packet, *I am referring to a complete PDU that includes header and footer information from all layers of the OSI model.*

Network Hardware

Now it's time to look at network hardware, where all of the dirty work is done. We'll focus on just a few of the more common pieces of network hardware—specifically, hubs, switches, and routers.

Hubs

A *hub* is generally no more than a box with multiple RJ-45 ports, like the Netgear hub shown in Figure 1-3. Hubs range from very small four-port hubs to larger 48-port ones designed for rack mounting in a corporate environment. Hubs are designed to connect network devices so that they can communicate.

Figure 1-3: A typical four-port Ethernet hub

A hub is nothing more than a repeating device operating on the physical layer of the OSI model. A *repeating device* simply takes packets sent from one port and transmits (repeats) them to every other port on the device. For example, if a computer on port one of a four-port hub needs to send data to a computer on port two, the hub sends those packets to ports one, two, three, and four. The clients connected to ports three and four ignore the data because it's not for them, and they drop (discard) the packets. The result is a lot of unnecessary network traffic.

Imagine you are sending an email to the employees of a company. The email has the subject line *Regarding all marketing staff*, but instead of sending it to only those people who work in the marketing department, you send it to every employee in the company. The employees who work in marketing will know it is for them, and they will open it. The other employees, however, will see that it is not for them, and will discard it. You can see how this would result in a lot of unnecessary communication and wasted time—yet this is exactly how a hub functions.

Figure 1-4 provides a graphical display of what is going on here. In this figure, computer A is transmitting data to computer B. However, when computer A sends this data, all computers connected to the hub receive it. Only computer B actually accepts the data; the other computers discard it.

One last note about hubs is that they are only capable of operating in *half-duplex mode*—that is, they cannot send and receive data at the same time. This differentiates them from switches, which are *full-duplex devices* that can send and receive data synchronously.

While you won't typically see hubs used in most modern or high-density networks (switches are used instead, as discussed below), you should know how hubs work, since they will be very important to packet analysis.

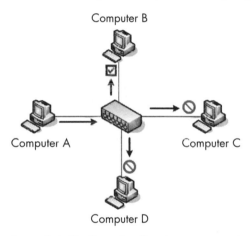

Figure 1-4: The flow of traffic when computer A transmits data to computer B through a hub

Switches

The best alternatives to hubs in a production or high-density network are devices called *switches*. Like a hub, a switch is designed to repeat packets, but it does so very differently; also like a hub, a switch provides a communication path for devices, but it does so more efficiently. Rather than broadcasting data to every individual port, a switch only sends data to the computer for which the data is intended. Physically speaking, a switch looks identical to a hub. As a matter of fact, if the device doesn't identify itself in writing on the front, you may have trouble knowing exactly which one it is (Figure 1-5).

Several of the larger switches on the market are manageable via special-ized, vendor-specific software or web interfaces. These switches are commonly referred to as *managed switches* and provide several features that can be useful in network management. This includes the ability to enable or disable specific ports, view port specifics, make configuration changes, and remotely reboot the switch.

Figure 1-5: A rack-mountable 24-port Ethernet switch

Switches have advanced functionality in handling transmitted packets. In order to be able to communicate directly with specific devices, switches must be able to uniquely identify devices based on their addresses. All this means that they must operate on the data link layer of the OSI model.

Switches store the Layer 2 address of every connected device in a *CAM table*, which acts as a kind of traffic cop. When a packet is transmitted, the switch reads the Layer 2 header information in the packet and, using the CAM table as reference, determines which port(s) to send the packet to. Switches only send packets to specific ports, which greatly reduces network traffic.

Figure 1-6 shows a graphical representation of traffic flow through a switch. In this figure, computer A is once again sending data to computer B. In this instance, the computers are connected through a switch that allows computer A to send data directly to computer B without the other devices on the network being aware of this communication. Moreover, multiple conver-sations can happen at the same time.

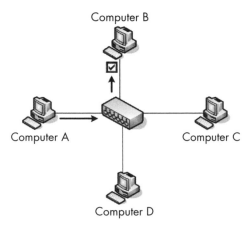

Figure 1-6: The flow of traffic when computer A transmits data to computer B through a switch

Routers

A *router* is an advanced network device with a much higher level of functionality than either a switch or a hub. A router can take many shapes and forms, but most have several LED indicator lights on the front and a few network ports on the back, depending on the size of the network (Figure 1-7). Routers operate at Layer 3 of the OSI model, where they are responsible for forwarding packets between two or more networks. The process routers use to direct the flow of traffic among networks is called *routing*.

There are several types of routing protocols that dictate how different types of packets are routed to other networks. Routers commonly use Layer 3 addresses (such as IP addresses) to uniquely identify devices on a network.

Figure 1-7: A small router suited for use in a small network

An easy way to illustrate the concept of routing is to think of a neighborhood with a network of streets; each street has houses on it, and each house has its own address (Figure 1-8). You live on a street, so you can move among all houses on the street. This is very similar to the operation of a switch that allows communication among all computers on a network segment. To communicate with a neighbor on another street, however, a person must follow the street signs to that neighbor's house.

Let's work through an example of communication across streets. Using Figure 1-8, let's say I am sitting at 503 Vine Street, and I need to get to 202 Dogwood Lane. In order to do this, I must cross onto Oak Street, and then onto Dogwood Lane. Think of this as crossing network segments. If the device at 192.168.0.3 needs to communicate with the device at 192.168.0.54, it must cross a router to get to the 10.100.1.1 network, then cross the destination network segment's router before it can get to the destination network segment.

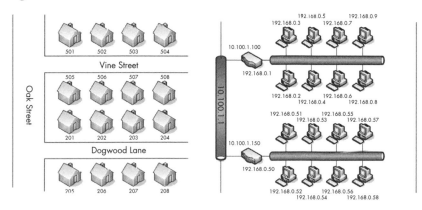

Figure 1-8: Comparison of a routed network to neighborhood streets

The size and number of routers on a network will depend on the size and function of that network. Personal and home-office networks may only consist of a small router located at the center of the network, whereas a large corporate network might have several routers spread throughout various departments, all connecting to one large central router or Layer 3 switch. A *Layer 3 switch* is an advanced type of switch that also has built-in functionality to act as a router.

As you begin looking at more and more network diagrams, you will come to understand how data flows through these various points. Figure 1-9 shows the layout of a very common form of routed network. In this example, two separate networks are connected via a single router. If a computer on network A wishes to communicate with a computer on network B, the transmitted data must go through the router.

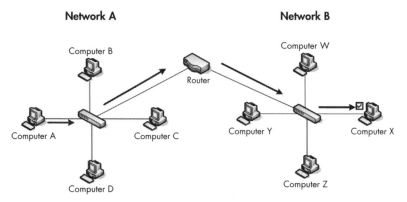

Figure 1-9: The flow of traffic when computer A transmits data to computer X through a router

Traffic Classifications

When considering network traffic, we break it into three main classes: broadcast, multicast, and unicast. Each classification has a distinct characteristic that determines how packets in that class are handled by networking hardware.

Broadcast Traffic

A *broadcast packet* is one that is sent to all ports on a network segment, regardless of whether that port is a hub, switch, or router. Remember from the section "Hubs" on page 8 that hubs are only capable of broadcast traffic.

Multicast Traffic

Multicast is a means of transmitting a packet from a single source to multiple destinations simultaneously. The goal of multicast is to make this process as simple as possible by using as little bandwidth as possible. The optimization of this traffic lies in the number of times a stream of data is replicated in order to get to its destination. The exact handling of multicast traffic is highly dependent upon its implementation in individual protocols. The primary method of implementing multicast is by using a special addressing scheme that joins the packet recipients to a multicast group; this is how IP multicast works. This addressing scheme ensures that the packets are not capable of being transmitted to computers they are not destined for.

Unicast Traffic

A *unicast packet* is transmitted from one computer directly to another. The details of how unicast functions depend upon the protocol using it.

Broadcast Domains

Recall that a broadcast packet is one that is sent to every device on a particular segment. In larger networks with multiple hubs or switches connected via different mediums, broadcast packets transmitted from one switch reach all the way to the ports on the other switches on the network, as they are repeated from switch to switch.

The extent to which broadcast packets travel is called the *broadcast domain*—it is the network segment where any computer can directly transmit to another computer without going through a router. Figure 1-10 shows an example of two broadcast domains on a small network. Because each broadcast domain extends until it reaches the router, broadcast packets circulate only within this specified broadcast domain.

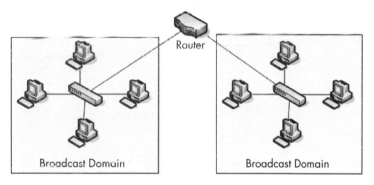

Figure 1-10: A broadcast domain extends to everything behind the current routed segment.

Our earlier example describing how routing relates to a neighborhood also provides good insight into how broadcast domains work. You can think of a broadcast domain as being like a neighborhood street. If you stand on your front porch and yell, only the people on your street will be able to hear you. If you want to talk to someone on a different street, you have to find a way to speak to that person directly, rather than broadcasting (yelling) from your front porch.

The things you have learned here are the absolute basics of packet analysis. You *must* understand what is going on at this level of network communication before you can begin troubleshooting network issues. In the next chapter we will build on these concepts and discuss more advanced network communication principles.

2

TAPPING INTO THE WIRE

We can now move on to the final step of preparation before we begin to capture live packets on the network. This last step is to figure out the most appropriate place to put a sniffer on the network's cabling system. This is most often referred to by packet analysts as *getting on the wire, tapping the network,* or *tapping into the wire*. Simply put, this is the process of placing a packet sniffer on a network in the correct physical location.

Unfortunately, sniffing packets is not as simple as plugging in a laptop to a network port and capturing traffic (Figure 2-1). In fact, it is sometimes more difficult to place a packet sniffer on a network's cabling system than it is to actually analyze the packets.

The challenge with sniffer placement is that there is a large variety of networking hardware that is used to connect devices. Because the three main devices on a modern network (hubs, switches, and routers) all handle traffic very differently, you must be very aware of the physical setup of the network you are analyzing.

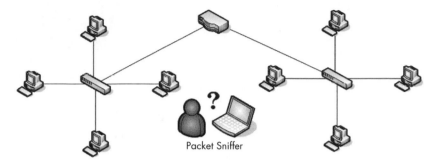

Packet Sniffer

Figure 2-1: Placing your sniffer on the network is sometimes the biggest challenge you will face.

The goal of this chapter is to help you develop an understanding of packet sniffer placement in a variety of different network topologies. We will look at various real-world network setups as we determine the best way to capture packets in hub-, switch-, and router-based environments. As a precursor to understanding sniffer placement, we'll also take a more in-depth look at promiscuous mode network cards, how they work, and why they are a necessity for packet analysis.

Living Promiscuously

Before you can sniff packets on a network, you need a network interface card (NIC) that supports a promiscuous mode driver. *Promiscuous mode* is what allows an NIC to view all of the packets crossing the cabling system.

When an NIC is not in promiscuous mode, it generally sees a large amount of broadcast and other traffic that is not addressed to it, which it will drop. When it is in promiscuous mode, it captures everything and passes all traffic it receives to the CPU, basically ignoring the information it finds in a packet's Layer 2 addresses. Your packet sniffing application grabs those packets to give you a complete and accurate account of all packets on the system.

NOTE   *Most operating systems (including Windows) will not let you use a network card in promiscuous mode unless you have elevated user privileges. If you cannot obtain these privileges on a system, chances are that you should not be performing any type of packet sniffing on that particular network.*

Sniffing Around Hubs

Sniffing on a network that has hubs installed is a dream for any packet analyst. As you learned earlier, traffic sent through a hub is sent to every port connected to that hub. Therefore, to analyze a computer on a hub, all you have to do is plug in a packet sniffer to an empty port on the hub, and you can see all communication to and from all computers connected to that hub. As illustrated in Figure 2-2, your visibility window is limitless when your sniffer is connected to a hub network.

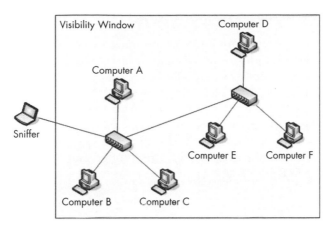

Figure 2-2: Sniffing on a hub network provides a limitless visibility window.

NOTE   *The visibility window, as shown in various diagrams throughout this book, shows the devices on the network whose traffic you are able to see with a packet sniffer.*

Unfortunately for us, hub-based networks are pretty rare because of the headache they cause network administrators. Hubs tend to slow network traffic because only one device can use the hub at any one time; therefore, a device connected through a hub must compete for bandwidth with the other devices also trying to communicate through it. When two or more devices communicate at the same time, packets collide (as shown in Figure 2-3) and transmitted packets are lost and have to be retransmitted.

As collisions increase, network performance can decrease dramatically. As the level of traffic and collisions increases, devices may have to transmit a packet three or four times, which is why most modern networks of any size use switches.

The only other concern you have to consider when sniffing the traffic of an individual computer on a hub network is the volume of traffic in your capture. Since an NIC in promiscuous mode sees all traffic going to and from all devices on a hub, you will have a very large amount of data to sort through, the bulk of which will be irrelevant. In the next chapter you'll learn how to leverage the power of capture and display filters in order to perform your analysis more efficiently.

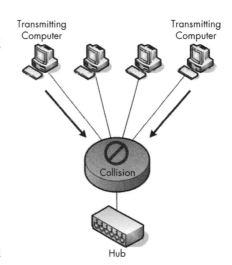

Figure 2-3: Collisions occur on a hub network when two devices transmit at the same time.

Sniffing in a Switched Environment

A switched environment is the most common type of network you will be working on. Switches provide an efficient means of transporting data via broadcast, unicast, and multicast traffic. (For more on these topics see Chapter 1.) As a bonus, switches allow full-duplex communication, meaning that machines can send and receive data simultaneously through a switch. Unfortunately for packet analysts, switches add a whole new level of complexity to a packet analyst's job. When you plug in a sniffer to a port on a switch, you can only see broadcast traffic and the traffic transmitted and received by your machine, as shown in Figure 2-4.

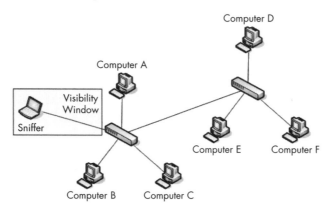

Figure 2-4: The visibility window on a switched network is limited to the port you are plugged into.

There are three primary ways to capture traffic from a target device on a switched network: port mirroring, ARP cache poisoning, and hubbing out.

Port Mirroring

Port mirroring, or *port spanning* as it is often called, is perhaps the easiest way to capture the traffic from a target device on a switched network. In this type of setup, you must have access to the command-line interface of the switch on which the target computer is located. Also, the switch must support port mirroring and have an empty port into which you can plug your analyzer.

When port mirroring, you log into the command-line interface for your switch and enter a command that forces the switch to copy all traffic on a certain port to another port (Figure 2-5). For instance, to capture the traffic from a device on port three of a switch, you could simply plug your analyzer into port four and mirror port three to port four. This would allow you to see all traffic transmitted and received by your target device.

The exact command you will type to set up port mirroring will vary depending on the manufacturer of the switch you are using. You'll find a list of common commands in Table 2-1.

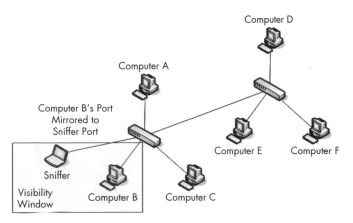

Figure 2-5: Port mirroring allows you to expand your visibility window
on a switched network.

When port mirroring, be aware of the throughput of the ports you are mirroring. Some switch manufacturers allow you to mirror multiple ports to one individual port, which may be very useful when analyzing the communication between two or more devices on a single switch. However, consider what will happen using some basic math. For instance, if you have a 24-port switch and you mirror 23 full-duplex 100Mbps ports to one port, you could potentially have 4,600Mbps flowing to that port. This is obviously well beyond the physical threshold of a single port and can cause packet loss or network slowdowns if the traffic reaches a certain level. In these situations switches have been known to completely drop excess packets or "pause" their backplane, preventing communication altogether. Be sure that this type of situation doesn't occur when you are when trying to perform your capture.

Table 2-1: Commands Used to Enable Port Mirroring for Different Manufacturers' Switches

Manufacturer	Port Mirroring Command
Cisco	set span <source port> <destination port>
Enterasys	set port mirroring create <source port> <destination port>
Nortel	port-mirroring mode mirror-port <source port> monitor-port <destination port>

Hubbing Out

Another very simple way of capturing the traffic through a target device on a switched network is by hubbing out. *Hubbing out* is a technique in which you localize the target device and your analyzer system on the same network segment by plugging them directly into a hub.

Many people think of hubbing out as cheating, but it's really a perfect solution in situations where you can't perform port mirroring but still have physical access to the switch the target device is plugged into.

In order to hub out, all you need is a hub and a few network cables. Once you have your hardware, go to the switch the target device resides on and unplug the target from the network. Then plug the target's network cable into your hub, and plug in another cable connecting your analyzer. Next, connect your hub to the network by plugging in a network cable from it to the network switch. Now you have basically put the target device and your analyzer into the same broadcast domain, and all traffic from your target device will be broadcast so that the analyzer can capture those packets (Figure 2-6).

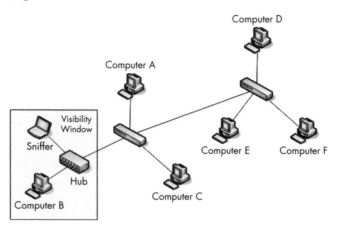

Figure 2-6: Hubbing out isolates your target device and analyzer on their own broadcast domain.

In most situations, hubbing out will reduce the duplex of the target device from full to half. While this method isn't the cleanest way to tap into the wire, it's sometimes your only option when a switch does not support port mirroring.

NOTE   *As a reminder, it is usually a nice gesture to alert the user of the device that you will be unplugging it, especially if that user happens to be the company CEO!*

When hubbing out, be sure that you're using a true hub and not a falsely labeled switch. Several networking hardware vendors have a bad habit of marketing and selling a device as a hub when it actually functions as a low-level switch. If you aren't working with a proven, tested hub, you will only see your own traffic, not that of the target device. When you find a hub, test it to make sure it really is a hub—if it is, it's a keeper! The best way to determine whether or not the device you are using is a true hub is to hook a pair of computers up to it and see if one can sniff the other's traffic. If so, you have a true hub in your possession.

ARP Cache Poisoning

Recall from Chapter 1 that the two main types of packet addressing are at Layers 2 and 3 of the OSI model. These Layer 2 addresses, or MAC addresses, are used in conjunction with whichever Layer 3 addressing system you are using. In the case of this book (and the industry standard), I refer to the Layer 3 addressing system as the Internet Protocol (IP) addressing system.

All devices on a network communicate with each other on Layer 3 using IP addresses. Because switches operate on Layer 2 of the OSI model, they must be able to translate Layer 2 MAC addresses into Layer 3 IP addresses and vice versa in order to be able to forward traffic to the appropriate device. This translation process is done through a Layer 3 protocol known as the *Address Resolution Protocol (ARP)*.

When one computer needs to send data to another, it sends an ARP request to the switch it is connected to. The switch then sends an ARP broadcast packet to all of the computers connected to it, asking each computer it reaches if it is has the IP address of the computer trying to be reached. When the destination computer sees this packet, it identifies itself to the switch by giving its MAC address. The switch now has a route established to that destination computer, and any device that wishes to communicate with the destination computer can use the route. This newly obtained information is stored in the switch's ARP cache so that the switch does not have to send a new ARP broadcast every time it needs to send data to a computer.

ARP cache poisoning is a more advanced form of tapping into the wire on a switched network. It is commonly used by hackers to send falsely addressed packets to client systems in order to intercept certain traffic or cause denial of service (DoS) attacks on a target, but ARP cache poisoning can still serve as a legitimate way to capture the packets of a target machine on a switched network.

ARP cache poisoning, sometimes referred to as *ARP spoofing*, is the process of sending ARP messages to an Ethernet switch or router with fake MAC (Layer 2) addresses in order to intercept the traffic of another computer (Figure 2-7).

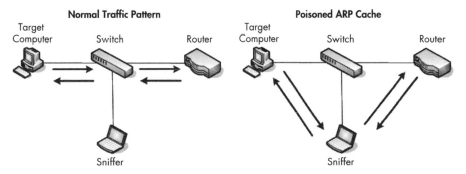

Figure 2-7: ARP cache poisoning allows you to intercept the traffic of your target computer.

Using Cain & Abel

When attempting to poison the ARP cache, the first step is to download the required tools and collect some necessary information. We'll use the popular security tool Cain & Abel from Oxid.it (http://www.oxid.it). Go ahead and install it now.

Once you have installed the Cain & Abel software, you need to collect some additional information including the IP addresses of your analyzer system, the remote system you wish to capture the traffic from, and the router that the remote system is downstream from.

When you first open Cain & Abel, you will notice a series of tabs near the top of the window. (ARP cache poisoning is only one of a variety of Cain & Abel's features.) For our purposes, we'll be working in the Sniffer tab. When you click this tab, you will see an empty table (Figure 2-8).

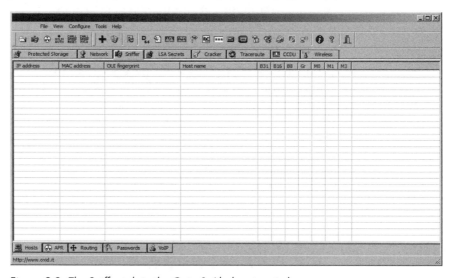

Figure 2-8: The Sniffer tab in the Cain & Abel main window

In order to fill this table you will need to activate the program's built-in sniffer and scan your network for hosts. To do so, follow these steps:

1. Click the second icon on the toolbar, which resembles a network card. The first time you do this you will be asked to select the interface you wish to sniff. This interface should be the one that is connected to the network you will be performing your ARP cache poisoning on.

2. Once you've selected this interface, click **OK** to activate Cain & Abel's built-in sniffer.

3. To build a list of available hosts on your network, click the icon that resembles a plus (+) symbol, and click **OK** (Figure 2-9).

The once-empty grid should now be filled with a list of all the hosts on your attached network, along with their MAC addresses, IP addresses, and vendor identifying information. This is the list you will work from when setting up your ARP cache poisoning.

At the bottom of the program window, you will see a set of tabs that will take you to other windows under the Sniffer heading. Now that you have built your host list, you will be working from the APR tab. Switch to the APR window by clicking the tab.

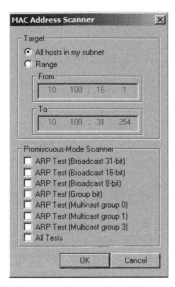

Figure 2-9: The Cain & Abel network discovery tool

Once in the APR window, you are presented with two empty tables: an upper and a lower one. Once you set them up, the upper table will show the devices involved in your ARP cache poisoning, and the lower table will show all communication between your poisoned machines.

To set up your poisoning, follow these steps:

1. Click the icon resembling the plus (+) symbol on the program's standard toolbar. The window that appears has two selection columns side by side.

2. On the left side, you will see a list of all available hosts on your network. Click the IP address of the target computer whose traffic you wish to sniff. This will result in the right window showing a list of all hosts in the network, omitting the target machine's IP address.

3. In the right window, click the IP address of the router that is directly upstream of the target machine, and click **OK** (Figure 2-10). The IP addresses of both devices should now be listed in the upper table in the main application window.

4. To complete the process, click the yellow-and-black radiation symbol on the standard toolbar. This will activate Cain & Abel's ARP cache poisoning features and allow your analyzing system to be the middleman for all communications between the target system and its upstream router.

You can now fire up your packet sniffer and begin the analysis process. When you are finished capturing traffic, simply click the yellow-and-black radiation symbol again to stop ARP cache poisoning.

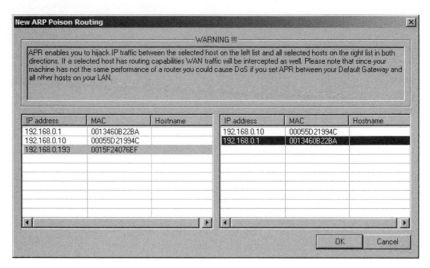

Figure 2-10: Selecting the devices for which you wish to enable ARP cache poisoning

NOTE *As a final note on ARP cache poisoning, you should be very aware of the roles of the systems you implement this process for. For instance, do not use this technique when the target device is something with very high network utilization, such as a fileserver with a 1Gbps link to the network (especially if your analyzer system only provides a 100Mbps link). When you perform this rerouting of traffic, all traffic transmitted and received by the target system must first go through your analyzer system, therefore making your analyzer the bottleneck in the communication process. This can create a DoS-type effect on the machine you are analyzing, which will result in degraded network performance and faulty analysis data.*

Sniffing in a Routed Environment

All of the techniques for tapping into the wire on a switched network are available on routed networks, as well. The only major consideration when dealing with routed environments is the importance of sniffer placement when you are troubleshooting a problem that spans multiple network segments.

As you learned earlier, a device's broadcast domain extends until it reaches a router. At this point the traffic is handed off to the next upstream router and you lose communication with the packets being transmitted until you receive an acknowledgment of their receipt. In situations like this where data must traverse multiple routers, it is important to analyze the traffic on all sides of the router.

For example, consider the communications problem you might encounter in a network with several network segments connected via a variety of routers. In this network, each segment communicates with an upstream segment in order to store and retrieve data. The problem we're trying to solve is that a downstream subnet, network D, cannot communicate with any devices on network A (Figure 2-11).

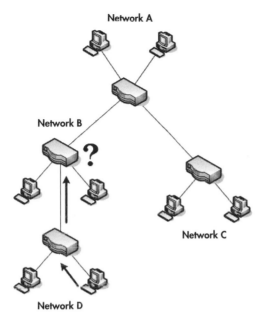

Figure 2-11: A computer on network D can't communicate with one on network A.

Your gut might tell you to sniff the traffic of a device on segment D. When you do, you can clearly see data being transmitted to segment A, but without traffic acknowledgments. When sniffing the next upstream network segment to find the source of the problem, you find that traffic is dropped by the router of network B. Eventually this leads you to a router configuration problem that, when corrected, solves your larger dilemma. This is a prime example of why it is often necessary to sniff the traffic of multiple devices on multiple segments in order to pinpoint a problem.

Network Maps

In our brief discussion about network placement, we have already looked at several different network maps. A *network map*, or *network diagram*, is a diagram showing all technical resources on a network and how they are connected.

There is no better way to determine the placement of your packet sniffer than to be able to visualize the network clearly. If you have a network map available to you, I would highly recommend keeping it handy, as it will become a valuable asset in the troubleshooting and analysis process. You may even want to make a detailed network map of your own network. Remember, sometimes half the battle in troubleshooting is pinpointing the problem.

3

INTRODUCTION TO WIRESHARK

There are several different packet sniffing applications available for performing network analysis, but we'll be using Wireshark throughout this book. This chapter discusses the history of Wireshark, as well as its benefits, installation, and basic use.

A Brief History of Wireshark

Wireshark has a very rich history. Gerald Combs, a computer science graduate of the University of Missouri at Kansas City, originally developed it out of necessity. The very first version of Combs' application, called Ethereal, was released in 1998 under the GNU Public License (GPL).

Eight years after releasing Ethereal, Combs left his job to pursue other career opportunities. Unfortunately, his employer at that time had full rights to the Ethereal trademarks, and Combs was unable to reach an agreement that would allow him to control the Ethereal "brand." Instead, Combs and the rest of the development team rebranded the project as *Wireshark* in mid-2006.

Wireshark has grown dramatically in popularity, and its collaborative development team now boasts over 500 contributors. The program as it exists under the Ethereal name is no longer being developed.

The Benefits of Wireshark

Wireshark offers several benefits that make it appealing for everyday use. It is aimed at both the journeyman and the expert packet analyst and offers a variety of features to entice each. Let's examine Wireshark according to the criteria I defined in Chapter 1 for selecting a packet sniffing tool.

Supported Protocols

Wireshark excels in the number of protocols that it supports—over 850 as of this writing. These protocols run from common ones like IP and DHCP to more advanced proprietary protocols like AppleTalk and BitTorrent. And because Wireshark is developed under an open source model, new protocol support is added with each update. If there is a protocol that Wireshark doesn't support, you can code that support yourself and submit your code to the Wireshark developers for inclusion in the application (if your code is accepted, of course). That said, there is really almost no protocol that Wireshark isn't capable of supporting.

User Friendliness

The Wireshark interface is one of the easiest to understand of any packet sniffing application. Wireshark is a GUI-based application with very clearly written context menus and a straightforward layout. It also provides several features designed to enhance usability, such as protocol-based color coding and detailed graphical representations of raw data. Unlike some of the more complicated command-line driven alternatives like tcpdump, the Wireshark GUI is great for those who are just entering the world of protocol analysis.

Cost

Since it is open source, Wireshark's pricing can't be beat. Wireshark is released as free software under the GPL. You can download and use Wireshark for any purpose, whether personal or commercial.

Program Support

A software package's level of support can make or break it. When dealing with freely distributed software such as Wireshark, there is often no formal support, which is why the open source community often relies on its user base to provide support. Luckily for us, the Wireshark community is one of the best and most active of any open source project. The Wireshark web page links directly to several forms of support, including online documentation, a support and development wiki, FAQs, and a place to sign up for the Wireshark mailing list, which is monitored by most of the program's top developers. These developers, along with Wireshark's massive user base, provide support that leaves no question unanswered.

Operating System Support

Wireshark supports all major modern operating systems, including Windows, Mac OS X, and Linux-based platforms. You can view a complete list of supported operating systems on the Wireshark home page.

Installing Wireshark

The Wireshark installation process is surprisingly simple. In this section we will look at Wireshark's system requirements and then go through the steps involved in installing Wireshark on both Windows and Linux.

System Requirements

Before you install Wireshark, you must make sure that your system meets the following requirements:

- A 400 MHz processor or faster
- At least 60MB of available storage space
- An NIC that supports promiscuous mode
- The WinPcap capture driver

The WinPcap capture driver is the Windows implementation of the Pcap packet capturing interface application programming interface (API). Simply put, this driver interacts with your OS to capture raw packet data, apply filters, and switch the NIC in and out of promiscuous mode. You can find the installation package for this driver at http://www.winpcap.org.

NOTE *Although you can download WinPcap separately, it is built into the Wireshark installation package. It is typically better to install WinPcap from the Wireshark installation package because the included version of WinPcap has been tested to work with Wireshark.*

Installing on Windows Systems

The first step when installing Wireshark under Windows is to obtain the latest installation build from the official Wireshark web page, http://www.wireshark.org. Navigate to the Downloads section on the website, and choose a mirror to download from. Once you've downloaded the package, follow these steps:

1. Double-click the .exe file to begin installation, and then click **Next** in the introductory window.
2. Read the licensing agreement and click **I Agree** if you agree.

3. Select the components of Wireshark you wish to install. For our purposes, you can accept the defaults by clicking **Next** (Figure 3-1).

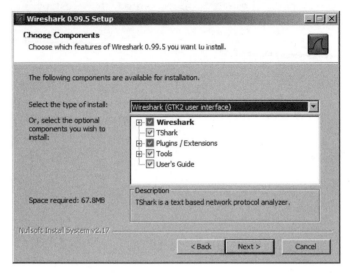

Figure 3-1: Choosing the Wireshark components you wish to install

4. Click **Next** in the Additional Tasks window.

5. Select the location where you wish to install Wireshark, and click **Next**.

6. When the dialog asks whether or not you want to install WinPcap, make sure the box next to the words *Install WinPcap* is checked, and click **Install** (Figure 3-2). The installation process should begin.

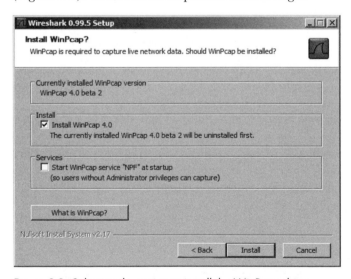

Figure 3-2: Selecting the option to install the WinPcap driver

7. About halfway through the Wireshark installation, the WinPcap installation should start. When it does, click **Next** in the introductory window. Then read the licensing agreement and click **I Agree** if you do.

8. WinPcap should install on your computer. Once it has finished, click **Finish**.

9. Wireshark should complete its installation. Once this is done, click **Next**.

10. Once the installation confirmation window appears, click **Finish**.

Installing on Linux Systems

The first step when installing Wireshark on a Linux system is to download the appropriate installation package. Not every version of Linux is supported, so don't be surprised if your specific distribution doesn't have its own install package.

RPM-based Systems

To install Wireshark on RPM-based distributions, such as Red Hat, do the following:

1. Download the appropriate installation package from the Wireshark web page.

2. Open a console window and type `rpm -ivh wireshark-0.99.3.i386.rpm`, substituting the filename of your downloaded package as appropriate.

3. If any dependencies are missing, install them and repeat the previous step.

DEB-based Systems

To install Wireshark on a DEB-based distribution such as Debian or Ubuntu, do the following:

1. Download the appropriate installation package from the Wireshark web page.

2. Open a console window and type `apt-get install wireshark`.

Wireshark Fundamentals

Once you've successfully installed Wireshark on your system, you can begin to familiarize yourself with it. Now you finally get to open your fully functioning packet sniffer and see . . . absolutely nothing!

The fact is, Wireshark isn't very interesting when you first open it. In order for things to really get exciting, you have to get some data.

Your First Packet Capture

In order to get packet data into Wireshark, you'll perform your first packet capture. You may be thinking, "How am I going to capture packets when nothing is wrong on the network?" There are two things wrong with this statement. The first thing is that there is *always* something wrong on the network. If you don't believe me, then go ahead and send an email to all of your employees and let them know that everything is working perfectly.

Secondly, there doesn't have to be something wrong in order for you to perform packet analysis. In fact, most packet analysts spend more time analyzing problem-free traffic than traffic they are troubleshooting; you need a baseline to compare to in order to be able to effectively troubleshoot network traffic. For example, if you ever hope to solve a problem with DHCP by analyzing its traffic, you must understand what the flow of working DHCP traffic looks like. More broadly, in order to find anomalies in daily network activity, you must know what normal daily network activity looks like. When your network is running smoothly, you can set your baseline so that you'll know what its traffic looks like in a normal state.

We've covered the basics. Now let's capture some packets!

1. Open Wireshark.

2. From the main drop-down menu, select **Capture** and then **Interfaces**. You should see a dialog listing the various interfaces that can be used to capture packets, along with their IP addresses. Choose the interface you wish to use, and click **Capture** (Figure 3-3).

Figure 3-3: Selecting an interface on which to perform your packet capture

3. Your packet capture should begin and Wireshark should show the active packet capture window. This window displays a brief summary of the type of traffic being captured, as well as the duration of the current capture (Figure 3-4).

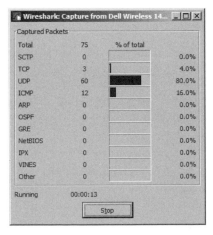

Figure 3-4: The Capture window shows a brief summary of the packets being captured.

4. Wait about a minute or so, and when you are ready to stop the capture and view your data, click **Stop**.

Once you have completed these steps and finished the capture process, the Wireshark main window will come alive with data. As a matter of fact, you might be overwhelmed by the amount of data that appears, but it will all start to make sense very quickly as we break down the main window of Wireshark one piece at a time.

The Main Window

You'll spend most of your time in the Wireshark main window. This is where all of the packets you capture are displayed and broken down into a more understandable format. Using the packet capture you just made, let's take a look at Wireshark's main window (Figure 3-5), which contains three panes.

The three panes in the main window depend upon one another. In order to view the details of an individual packet in the Packet Details pane, you must first select that packet by clicking on it in the Packet List pane. Once you've selected your packet, you can see the exact bytes that correspond with a certain portion of the packet in the Packet Bytes pane when you click that portion of the packet in the Packet Details pane.

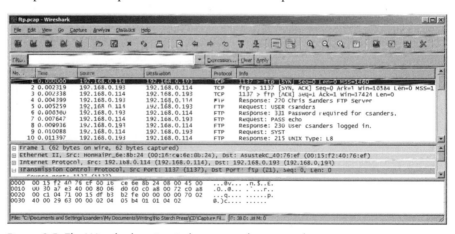

Figure 3-5: The Wireshark main window uses a three-pane design.

Packet List Pane

The top pane, known as the *Packet List pane*, displays a table containing all packets in the current capture file. You'll see columns containing the packet number, the relative time the packet was captured, the source and destination of the packet, the packet's protocol, and some general information found in the packet.

Packet Details Pane

The middle pane, known as the *Packet Details pane*, contains a hierarchical display of information about a single packet. This display can be collapsed and expanded to show all of the information collected about an individual packet.

Packet Bytes Pane

The lower pane, and perhaps the most confusing, is the *Packet Bytes pane.* This pane displays a packet in its raw, unprocessed form—that is, it shows what the packet looks like as it travels across the wire. This is raw information with nothing warm or fuzzy to make it easier to follow.

NOTE   *It is very important to understand how these different panes work with each other, since you will be spending most of your time working with them in the main window.*

The Preferences Dialog

Wireshark has several preferences that can be customized to meet your needs. Let's look at some of the more important ones.

To access Wireshark's preferences, select **Edit** from the main drop-down menu and click **Preferences**. This should call up the Preferences dialog, which contains several customizable options (Figure 3-6).

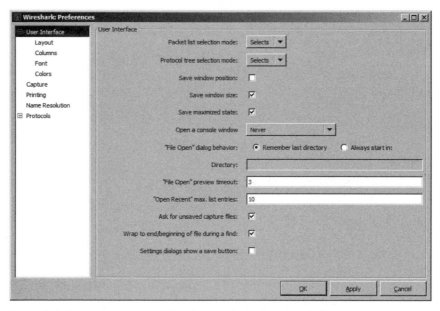

Figure 3-6: You can customize Wireshark in the Preferences dialog.

These preferences are divided into five major sections: user interface, capture, printing, name resolution, and protocols.

User Interface

The user interface preferences determine how Wireshark presents data. You can change most options here according to your personal preferences, including whether or not to save window positions, the layout of the three main panes, the placement of the scrollbar, the placement of the Packet List pane columns, the fonts used to display the captured data, and the background and foreground colors.

Capture

The capture preferences allow you to specify options related to the way packets are captured, including your default capture interface, whether or not to use promiscuous mode by default, and whether or not to update the Packet List pane in real time.

Printing

The printing preferences section allows you to specify various options related to the way Wireshark prints your data.

Name Resolution

The preferences in the name resolution section allow you to activate features of Wireshark that allow it to resolve addresses into more recognizable names (including MAC, network, and transport name resolution) and specify the maximum number of concurrent name resolution requests.

Protocols

The preferences in the protocols section allow you to manipulate options related to the capturing and display of the various protocols Wireshark is capable of decoding. Not every protocol has configurable preferences, but some have several things that can be changed. These options are best left unchanged unless you have a specific reason for doing so, however.

Packet Color Coding

If you are anything like me, you may have an aversion to shiny objects and pretty colors. If that is the case, the first thing you probably noticed when you opened Wireshark were the different colors of the packets in the Packet List pane (Figure 3-7). It may seem like these colors are randomly assigned to each individual packet, but this is not the case.

NOTE   *Whenever I refer to traffic, you can assume I am referring to all of the packets displayed in the Packet List pane. More specifically, when I refer to it in the context of DNS traffic, I am talking about all of the DNS protocol packets in the Packet List pane.*

Each packet is displayed as a certain color for a reason. For example, you may notice that all DNS traffic is blue and all HTTP traffic is green. These colors reflect the packet's protocol. The color coding allows you to quickly differentiate among various protocols so that you don't have to read the protocol field in the Packet List pane for each individual packet. You will find that this greatly speeds up the time it takes to browse through large capture files.

No. ▾	Time	Source	Destination	Protocol	Info
1 0.000000		10.100.17.47	10.100.16.15	DCERPC	Request: call_id: 95 opnum: 69 ctx_id: 0
2 0.000361		10.100.16.15	10.100.17.47	DCERPC	Response: call_id: 95 ctx_id: 0
3 0.001946		10.100.17.47	10.100.16.15	DCERPC	Request: call_id: 96 opnum: 26 ctx_id: 0
4 0.002034		10.100.16.15	10.100.17.47	DCERPC	Response: call_id: 96 ctx_id: 0

Figure 3-7: Wireshark's color coding allows for quick protocol identification.

Wireshark makes it easy to see which colors are assigned to each protocol through the Coloring Rules window. To open this window, follow these steps:

1. Open Wireshark.
2. Select **View** from the main drop-down menu.
3. Click **Coloring Rules**. The Coloring Rules window should appear (Figure 3-8), displaying a complete list of all the coloring rules defined within Wireshark. You can define your own coloring rules and modify existing ones.

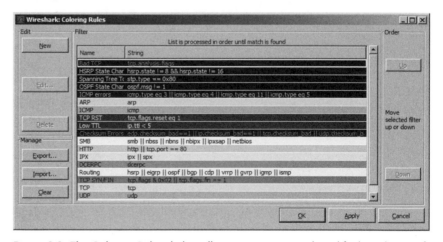

Figure 3-8: The Coloring Rules dialog allows you to view and modify the coloring of packets.

For example, to change the color used as the background for HTTP traffic from the default green to lavender, follow these steps:

1. Open Wireshark and access the Coloring Rules dialog (**View ▸ Coloring Rules**).

2. Find the HTTP coloring rule in the coloring rules list, and select it by clicking it once.

3. Click the **Edit** button.

4. Click the **Background Color** button (Figure 3-9).

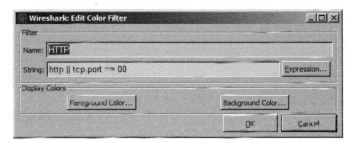

Figure 3-9: When editing a color filter, you can modify both foreground and background color.

5. Select the color you wish to use on the color wheel and click **OK**.

6. Click **OK** twice more to accept the changes and return to the main window.

7. The main window should then reload itself to reflect the updated color scheme.

As you work with Wireshark on your network, you will begin to notice that you work with certain protocols more than others. Here's where color-coded packets can make your life a lot easier. For example, if you think that there is a rogue DHCP server on your network handing out IP leases, you could simply modify the coloring rule for the DHCP protocol so that it shows up in bright yellow or some other easily identifiable color. This would allow you to pick out all DHCP traffic much more quickly and make your packet analysis more efficient.

4

WORKING WITH CAPTURED PACKETS

Now that you've performed your first packet capture, we'll cover a few more basic concepts that you need to know about working with those captured packets in Wireshark. This includes finding and marking packets, saving capture files, merging capture files, printing packets, and changing time display formats.

Finding and Marking Packets

Once you really get into doing packet analysis, you will eventually encounter scenarios involving a very large number of packets. As the number of these packets grows into the thousands and even millions, you will need to be able to navigate through packets more efficiently. This is the reason Wireshark allows you to find and mark packets that match certain criteria.

Finding Packets

To find packets that match particular criteria, open the Find Packet dialog (shown in Figure 4-1) by either selecting **Edit** from the main drop-down menu and then clicking **Find Packet** or pressing CTRL-F on your keyboard.

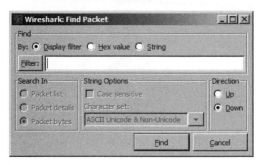

Figure 4-1: Finding packets in Wireshark based on specified criteria

This dialog offers three options for finding packets: display filter, hex value, or string. The display filter option allows you to enter an expression-based filter that will only find packets that satisfy that expression (this will be covered later). The hex and string value options search for packets with a hexadecimal or text string you specify; you can see examples of all these things in Table 4-1. Other options include the ability to select the window in which you want to search, the character set to use, and the direction in which you wish to search.

Table 4-1: Examples of Various Search Types for Finding Packets

Search Type	Example
Display filter	not ip, ip address==192.168.0.1, arp
Hex value	00:ff, ff:ff, 00:AB:B1:f0
String	Workstation1, UserB, domain

Once you've made your selections, enter your search string in the text box, and click **Find** to find the first packet that meets your criteria. To find the next matching packet, press CTRL-N, or find the previous matching packet by pressing CTRL-B.

Marking Packets

Once you have found the packets that match your criteria, you can mark those of particular interest. Marked packets stand out with a black background and white text, as shown in Figure 4-2. (You can also sort out only marked packets when saving packet captures.) There are several reasons you may want to mark a packet, including being able to save those packets separately, or to be able to find them quickly based upon the coloration.

No. ▾	Time	Source	Destination	Protocol	Info
1	0.000000	10.100.17.47	10.100.16.15	DCERPC	Request: call_id: 95 opnum: 69 ctx_id: 0
2	0.000361	10.100.16.15	10.100.17.47	DCERPC	Response: call_id: 95 ctx_id: 0

Figure 4-2: Comparison of a marked packet to an unmarked packet. They will be highlighted in different colors on your screen. In this example, packet 1 is marked.

To mark a packet, right-click it in the Packet List pane and choose **Mark Packet** from the pop-up. Or, single click a packet in the Packet List pane and press CTRL-M to mark it. To unmark a packet, toggle this setting off using CTRL-M again. You may mark as many packets as you wish in a capture. You can jump forward and backward between marked packets by pressing SHIFT-CTRL-N and SHIFT-CTRL-B, respectively.

Saving and Exporting Capture Files

As you perform packet analysis, you will find that a good portion of the analysis you do will happen after your capture. Usually, you will perform several captures at various times, save them, and analyze them all at once. Therefore, Wireshark allows you to save your capture files to be analyzed later.

Saving Capture Files

To save a packet capture, select **File** from the drop-down menu and then click **Save As**, or press SHIFT-CTRL hyphen. You should see the Save File As dialog (Figure 4-3). Here you will be prompted for a location to save your packet capture and for the file format you wish to use. If you do not specify a file format, Wireshark will use the default .pcap file format.

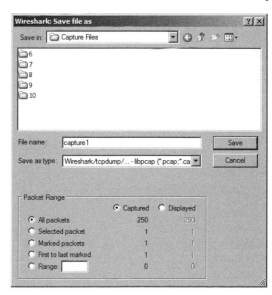

Figure 4-3: The Save File As dialog allows you to save your packet captures.

One of the more powerful features of the Save File As dialog is the ability to save a specific packet range. You can choose to save only packets in a specific number range, marked packets, or packets visible as the result of a display filter. This is a great way to thin bloated packet capture files.

Exporting Capture Data

You can export your Wireshark capture data into several different formats for viewing in other mediums or for importing into other packet-analysis tools. Formats include plaintext, PostScript, comma-separated value (CSV), and XML. To export your packet capture, choose **File ▶ Export**, and then select the format you wish to export to. You will be prompted with a Save As window containing options related to that specific format.

Merging Capture Files

Certain types of analysis require the ability to merge multiple capture files, and luckily, Wireshark provides two different methods for doing this.

To merge a capture file, follow these steps:

1. Open one of the capture files you want to merge.
2. Choose **File ▶ Merge** to bring up the Merge with Capture File dialog (Figure 4-4).
3. Select the new file you wish to merge into the already open file, and then select the method to use for merging the files. You can prepend the selected file to the currently open one, append it, or merge the files chronologically based on their timestamps.

Figure 4-4: The Merge with Capture File dialog allows you to merge two capture files.

Alternately, if you want to merge several files quickly in chronological order, consider using drag and drop. To do so, open the first capture file in Windows Explorer (or whatever your preferred file browser may be). Then browse to the second file, click it, and drag it into the Wireshark main window.

Printing Packets

Although most analysis will take place on the computer screen, you will still find the need to print captured data. To print captured packets, open the Print dialog by choosing **File ▶ Print** from the main menu (Figure 4-5).

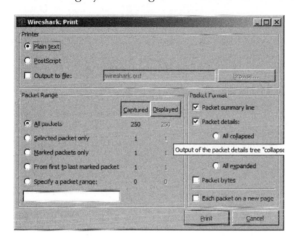

Figure 4-5: The Print dialog allows you to print the packets you specify.

You can print the selected data as plaintext, PostScript, or to an output file. As with the Save File As dialog, you can specify that it print a specific packet range, marked packets only, or packets displayed as the result of a filter. You can also select which of Wireshark's three main panes to print for each packet. Once you have selected the options you want, simply click **Print**.

Time Display Formats and References

Time is of the essence—especially in packet analysis. Everything that happens on a network is time sensitive, and you will need to examine trends and network latency in nearly every capture file. Wireshark recognizes the importance of time and supplies us with several configurable options relating to it. Here we take a look at time display formats and references.

Time Display Formats

Each packet that Wireshark captures is given a timestamp, which is applied to the packet by the operating system. Wireshark can show the absolute timestamp as well as the time in relation to the last captured packet and the beginning and end of the capture.

The options related to the time display are found under the View heading on the main menu. The Time Display Format section (shown in Figure 4-6) lets you configure the presentation format as well as the precision of the time display. The presentation format option lets you choose various options for time display. The precision options allow you to set the time display precision to Automatic or a manual setting such as seconds, milliseconds, microseconds, and so on. We will be changing these options very often later in the book, so you should familiarize yourself with them now.

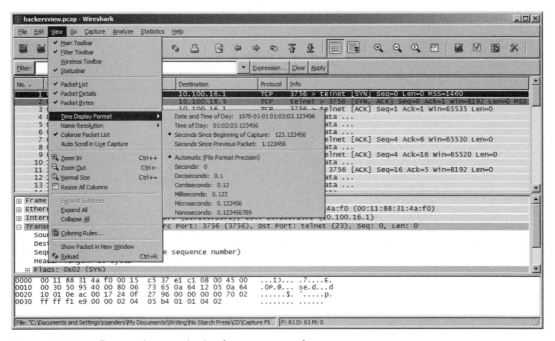

Figure 4-6: We will revisit the time display format options often.

Packet Time Referencing

Packet time referencing allows you to configure a certain packet so that all subsequent time calculations are done in relation to that specific packet. This feature is particularly handy when you are examining multiple data requests in one capture file and want to see packet times in reference to each individual request.

To set a time reference to a certain packet, select the reference packet in the Packet List pane, then choose **Edit ▶ Set Time Reference** from the main menu. Or, select the reference packet and press CTRL-T on your keyboard. To remove a time reference from a certain packet, select the packet and complete the aforementioned process a second time.

When you enable a time reference on a particular packet, the time column in the Packet List pane will display *REF* (Figure 4-7).

No. .	Time	Source	Destination	Protocol	Info
3	0.001263	10.100.18.5	10.100.16.1	TCP	3756 > telnet [ACK] Seq=1 Ack=1 Win=65535 Len=0
4	*REF*	10.100.16.1	10.100.18.5	TELNET	Telnet Data ...
5	0.000058	10.100.18.5	10.100.16.1	TELNET	Telnet Data ...
6	0.001018	10.100.16.1	10.100.18.5	TELNET	Telnet Data ...

Figure 4-7: A packet with the packet time reference toggle enabled

NOTE   *Setting a packet time reference is only useful when the time display format of a capture is set to display the time in relation to the beginning of the capture. Any other setting will produce no usable results and will create a set of times that can be very confusing.*

Capture and Display Filters

Earlier we discussed saving packets based upon filters. *Filters* allow us to show only particular packets in a given capture. We can create and use an expression to find exactly what we want in even the largest of capture files. An expression is no more than a string of text that tells Wireshark what to show and what not to show.

Wireshark offers two types of filters: capture filters and display filters.

Capture Filters

Capture filters are used during the actual packet capturing process, and are applied by WinPcap. Knowledge of their syntax can be useful in other network analysis programs, as well. You can configure them in the Capture Options dialog where you can specify which traffic you want or don't want to be captured.

One good way to use a capture filter would be when capturing traffic on a server with multiple roles. For example, suppose you are troubleshooting an issue with a service running on port 262. If the server you are analyzing runs several different services on a variety of ports, then finding and analyzing only the traffic on port 262 can be quite a job in itself. To capture only the port 262 traffic, you can use a capture filter. Just follow these steps:

1. Open the Capture Options dialog (Figure 4-8), select the interface you wish to capture packets on, and choose a capture filter.

2. You can apply the capture filter by typing an expression next to the Capture Filter button or by clicking the Capture Filter button itself, which will start the capture filter expression builder that will aid you in creating your filter. We want our filter to show only traffic inbound and outbound to port 262, so we type **port 262**, as shown in Figure 4-8.

3. Once you have set your filter, click **Start** to begin the capture. After collecting an adequate sample, you should now only see the port 262 traffic and be able to more efficiently analyze this particular data.

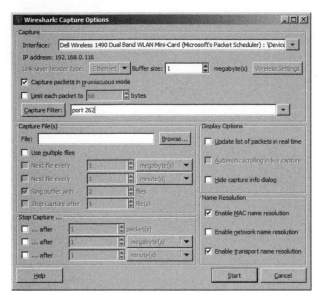

Figure 4-8: Creating a capture filter in the Capture Options dialog

Display Filters

A *display filter* is a filter that is applied to a capture file once that file has been created, that tells it to display only packets that match that filter. You can enter a display filter in the filter text box above the Packet List pane.

Display filters are more commonly used than capture filters because they allow you to filter packet data without actually omitting the rest of the data in the capture file. That way, if you need to revert back to the original capture, you can simply clear the filter expression.

You might use a display filter to clear irrelevant broadcast traffic from a capture file—for instance, to clear ARP broadcasts from the Packet List pane when these packets don't relate to the current problem being analyzed. However, because those ARP broadcast packets may be useful later, it's better to filter them temporarily than it is to delete them altogether.

To filter out all ARP packets in the capture window, follow these steps:

1. Navigate to the top of the Packet List pane and place your cursor in the Filter text box.

2. Type !arp and press ENTER to remove all ARP packets from the Packet List pane (Figure 4-9). To remove the filter, clear the textbox and press ENTER again.

Figure 4-9: Creating a display filter using the Filter text box above the Packet List pane.

The Filter Expression Dialog (the Easy Way)

The Filter Expression dialog (Figure 4-10) is a feature that makes it easy for novice Wireshark users to create capture and display filters. To access this dialog, click the **Capture Filter** button in the Capture Options dialog and then click the **Expression** button.

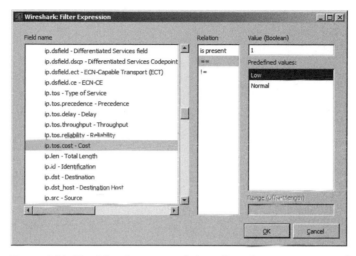

Figure 4-10: The Filter Expression dialog allows for easy creation of filters in Wireshark.

The first thing you will notice in the Filter Expression dialog is a list of all possible protocol fields on the left side of the window. These fields specify all possible filter criteria. To create a filter, follow these steps:

1. To view the specific criteria fields associated with a protocol, expand that protocol by clicking the plus (+) symbol next to it. Once you find the criteria you want to base your filter on, select it by clicking it.
2. Select the relation that the field you have selected will have to the criteria value you supply. This relation is specified in terms of equal to, greater than, less than, and so on.
3. Create your filter expression by specifying a criteria value that will relate to the field you selected. You can define this value or select it from predefined values programmed into Wireshark.
4. Once you have done this, click **OK** to view the completed text-only version of the filter you have just created.

The Filter Expression Syntax Structure (the Hard Way)

The Filter Expression dialog is great for novice users, but once you get the hang of things, you will find that manually typing filter expressions greatly increases their efficiency.

The display filter expression syntax structure is very simple, yet it is extremely powerful. This language is specific to Wireshark. Let's look at how this filter syntax works and some examples of what we can do with it.

Filtering Specific Protocols

You will most often use a capture or display filter to filter based upon a specific protocol. For example, say you are troubleshooting a TCP problem and you want to see only TCP traffic in a capture file. If so, simply using a filter of tcp will get the job done.

Now let's look at things from the other side of the fence. Imagine that in the course of troubleshooting your TCP problem, you have used the ping utility quite a bit, thereby generating a lot of ICMP traffic. You could remove this ICMP traffic from your capture file with the filter expression !icmp.

Comparison Operators

Comparison operators allow us to compare values. For example, when troubleshooting TCP/IP networks, you will often need to view all packets referencing a particular IP address. In a case like this, the equals (==) comparison operator will allow you to create a filter showing all packets with an IP address of 192.168.0.1 using a filter expression like ip.addr==192.168.0.1.

Or, consider this more advanced example of a comparison operator. Imagine a scenario where we only need to view the packets less than 128 bytes in length. We can use the less than or equal to (<=) operator to accomplish this goal in a filter expression like frame.pkt_len <= 128.

You'll find a complete list of Wireshark's comparison operators in Table 4-2.

Table 4-2: Wireshark Filter Expression Comparison Operators

Operator	Description
==	Equal to
!=	Not equal to
>	Greater than
<	Less than
>=	Greater than or equal to
<=	Less than or equal to

Logical Operators

Logical operators allow us to combine multiple filter expressions into one single statement. You can use logical operators to dramatically increase the effectiveness of your filters.

For example, consider our previous example of displaying only packets referencing a certain IP address, and now assume we are interested in two IP addresses. We can use the or operator to create one expression that will display packets containing either IP address. The syntax of this expression would be ip.addr==192.168.0.1 or ip.addr==192.168.0.2. You'll find a complete list of Wireshark's logical operators in Table 4-3.

Table 4-3: Wireshark Filter Expression Logical Operators

Operator	Description
and	Both conditions must be true
or	Either one of the conditions must be true
xor	One and only one condition must be true
not	Neither one of the conditions is true

Sample Filter Expressions

Although the concepts related to creating filter expressions are fairly simple, you will need to reference several specific keywords and operators when creating new filters for various problems. Because this book is not intended as a Wireshark user manual, we won't cover all of those keywords and operators, but you will find information on them at the Wireshark website. Table 4-4 gives you an idea of some sample filter expressions.

Table 4-4: Sample Capture and Display Filter Expressions

Expression	Description
host www.example.com	Displays all traffic from the host www.example.com
host www.example.com and not (port 80)	Displays all non-web traffic from the host www.example.com
!dns	Shows everything except DNS traffic
not broadcast and not multicast	Only shows unicast traffic
ip.dst==192.168.0.1	Shows all traffic destined for 192.168.0.1

Saving Filters

Once you begin creating lots of capture and display filters, you will find that you use certain ones frequently. Fortunately, you don't need to type these in each time you want to use them; Wireshark lets you save your filters for later use.

To save your custom filter, follow these steps:

1. Select **Capture ▸ Capture Filters** to open the Display Filter dialog (Figure 4-11).
2. Create a new filter by clicking the **New** button on the left side of the screen.
3. Type a name for your filter in the box next to the words *Filter name*.
4. Type the actual filter in the box next to the words *Filter string*.

5. Once you have finished, click the **Save** button to save your filter expression in the list.

Figure 4-11: The Display Filter dialog allows you to save filter expressions.

Wireshark also includes several built-in filters, but these are just to give you an example of what a filter should look like. You will want to use them when you are creating your own filters, however, because they are great for reference purposes.

5

ADVANCED WIRESHARK FEATURES

Once you master the basic concepts of Wireshark, you will probably want to delve further into some of its more advanced features. In this chapter we'll look at some of these powerful features, including name resolution, protocol dissection, and packet reassembly.

Name Resolution

Network data is transported via various alphanumeric addressing systems that are often too long or complicated to remember, such as the physical hardware address 00:16:CE:6E:8B:24. *Name resolution* (also called *name lookup*) is the process a protocol uses to convert one identifying address into another. For example, while a computer might have the physical address 00:16:CE:6E:8B:24, the DNS and ARP protocols allow us to see its name as Marketing-2. By associating easy-to-read names with these cryptic addresses, we make them easier to remember and identify.

We can leverage various name resolution tools to make our capture files more readable and to save a lot of time in certain situations. For example, we can use DNS name resolution to help readily identify the name of a computer we are trying to pinpoint as the source of a particular packet.

Types of Name Resolution Tools in Wireshark

There are three types of name resolution available in Wireshark: MAC name resolution, network name resolution, and transport name resolution.

MAC Name Resolution

MAC name resolution uses the ARP protocol to attempt to convert Layer 2 MAC addresses, such as 00:09:5B:01:02:03, into Layer 3 addresses, such as 10.100.12.1. If attempts at these conversions fail, Wireshark's last resort is to convert the first three bytes of the MAC address into the device's IEEE-specified manufacturer name, such as Netgear_01:02:03.

Network Name Resolution

Network name resolution attempts to convert a Layer 3 address, such as the IP address 192.168.1.50, into an easy-to-read DNS name such as MarketingPC1.

Transport Name Resolution

Transport name resolution attempts to convert a port number into a name associated with it. An example of this would be to display port 80 as *http*.

Enabling Name Resolution

To enable name resolution, open the Capture Options dialog (shown in Figure 5-1) either by choosing **Capture ▸ Options** or by pressing CTRL-K.

Potential Drawbacks to Name Resolution

Figure 5-1: Enabling name resolution features in the Capture Options dialog

Given its benefits, using name resolution may seem like a no-brainer, but there are some potential drawbacks, including the following:

- Sometimes name resolution fails. This may be simply because the name is unknown by the name server the query was sent to.

- Name resolution must take place every time you open a specific capture file because this information is not saved in the file. This means that if the servers that a file's name resolution depends upon are not available, name resolution will fail.
- DNS may add additional packets to the capture file, silently and without warning. The resulting traffic to resolve all DNS-based addresses will cloud your capture file.
- Name resolution requires additional processing overhead. If you are dealing with a very large capture file and are running low on memory, you may want to forgo the name resolution feature in order to conserve system resources.

Protocol Dissection

A *protocol dissector* allows Wireshark to break down a protocol (ICMP, for example) into various sections so that it can be analyzed. The ICMP protocol dissector allows Wireshark to take the raw data off the wire and format it as an ICMP packet. You can think of a dissector as the translator between the raw data flowing across the wire and the Wireshark program. In order for a protocol to be supported by Wireshark, it must have a dissector built into it.

Wireshark uses several dissectors in unison to interpret each packet. It determines which dissectors to use by using its programmed logic and making a very well-educated guess.

Unfortunately, Wireshark does not always make the right choices when selecting the correct dissector to use on a packet. This is especially true when it is using a protocol on the network in a nonstandard configuration, such as a non-default port. Luckily, we can change the way Wireshark implements certain dissectors.

For example, open the trace file wrongdissector.dmp. Notice that this file contains a bunch of NetBIOS communication between two computers. However, there is something definitely wrong here. If you click a few of the packets, you will notice some data in the Packet Bytes pane that definitely does not look like NetBIOS traffic. In fact, if you look at packets 6 and 7, you can actually see a username and password being sent from one computer to the other.

After a little further investigation, we find that the computers we are analyzing are actually communicating via FTP (note the words *FTP Server* at the right side of Figure 5-2). Wireshark thinks that this is NetBIOS traffic because the server and client are configured to use FTP on port 137, the default port for NetBIOS communication.

```
0000  08 00 46 15 4c c0 00 20   78 e1 5a 80 08 00 45 00    ..F.L..  x.Z...E.
0010  00 63 6a eb 40 00 80 06   e1 c7 cf 89 07 67 cf 89    .cj.@...  .....g..
0020  07 68 00 89 05 04 d6 64   6e c9 ba 6c d9 1b 50 18    .h.....d  n..l..P.
0030  44 2b d3 1b 00 00 32 31   35 20 4d 53 44 4f 53 20    D+....21  5 MSDOS
0040  41 20 4e 20 28 46 54 50   53 65 72 76 65 72 20 56    A N (FTP  Server V
0050  33 2e 35 20 62 79 20 42   69 73 6f 6e 57 61 72 65    3.5 by B  isonWare
0060  20 49 6e 74 65 72 6e 61   74 69 6f 6e 61 6c 29 0d     Interna  tional).
0070  0a 00 00 00 00                                       .....
```

Figure 5-2: FTP server software? This can't be NetBIOS traffic!

To fix this problem, we force Wireshark to use the FTP protocol dissector on these packets, a process referred to as a *forced decode*. To perform this process, follow these steps:

1. Right-click one of the packets and select **Decode As**. This will bring up a dialog in which you can select the dissector you wish to use (Figure 5-3).

2. Tell Wireshark to decode all TCP source port 137 traffic using the FTP dissector by selecting **source (137)** from the drop-down menu and then selecting **FTP** under the Transport tab.

3. Once you have made your selections, click **OK** to see the changes immediately applied to the capture file. You should see the data nicely decoded so that you can analyze it from the Packet List pane without having to dig deep into its individual bytes.

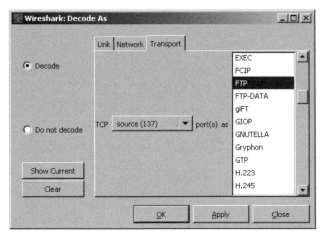

Figure 5-3: The Decode As dialog allows you to create forced decodes.

NOTE   *The changes you make when creating a forced decode are not saved when you save the capture file. You must recreate your forced decodes every time you open the capture file.*

You can use this feature multiple times within the same capture file. Because it can be hard to keep track of the forced decodes you have applied when you use more than one in a capture file, Wireshark does so for you. From the Decode As dialog, you can click the Show Current button to display all of the forced decodes you have created so far. You can also clear them by clicking the Clear button (Figure 5-4).

Figure 5-4: Clicking the Show button shows all of the forced decodes you have created for a capture file.

Following TCP Streams

One of Wireshark's most useful analysis features is its ability to view TCP streams as the application layer sees them. This feature allows you to combine all the information related to packets and shows you the data that those packets are handing off to the applications that the end user sees. Rather than viewing data being sent from client to server in a bunch of small chunks, the TCP Stream feature sorts the data to make it easily viewable.

You could use this tool when trying to capture and decipher instant messages sent by an employee who is suspected of giving away corporate accounting information. To see how this would work, open the example file suspectemployeechat.dmp. In this file you will see a large amount of traffic generated by the popular IM client MSN Messenger. (You can identify this as MSN Messenger traffic by the *MSNMS* that appears in the protocol field in the Packet List pane.)

If you examine the details of each packet, you can see small bits of text being transmitted in each one. We could spend a lot of time writing down the information from each packet and combining it to find out what is being said in the chat, but that isn't too practical. Instead, we will use the TCP Stream window to get a better picture of what is going on.

To follow the TCP stream data, right-click a packet and select **Follow TCP Stream**. Doing this in the example capture file will yield some very positive results. The TCP Stream window now shows the complete chat between our suspect employee and the person he is communicating with (Figure 5-5).

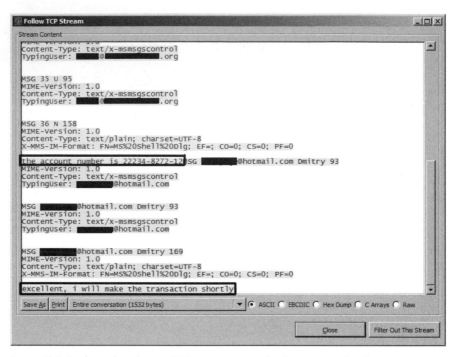

Figure 5-5: Looking directly at a TCP stream can make the picture a lot clearer.

In addition to viewing the data in this window, you can also save it as a text file, print it, or choose to view the data in ASCII, EBCDIC, Hex, C Arrays, or raw data format.

The Protocol Hierarchy Statistics Window

When dealing with extremely large capture files, we sometimes need to determine the distribution of protocols in the file—that is, what percentage of a capture is TCP, what percentage is IP, what percentage is DHCP, and so on. Rather than counting each packet and totaling the results, we can use Wireshark's Protocol Hierarchy Statistics window. This is a great way to benchmark your network. For instance, if you know that 10 percent of your network traffic is usually made up of ARP traffic, and one day you take a capture that is 50 percent ARP traffic, then you know something might be wrong.

Open the Protocol Hierarchy Statistics window (shown in Figure 5-6) by choosing **Statistics ▶ Protocol Hierarchy**.

Notice that not all totals add up to exactly 100 percent. Because a lot of the packets you will see contain multiple protocols from various layers, the count of each protocol as compared to each packet may be off. Nevertheless, you will still get an accurate view of the distribution of protocols in the capture file.

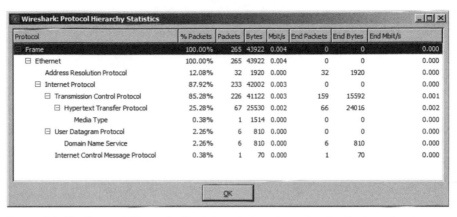

Protocol	% Packets	Packets	Bytes	Mbit/s	End Packets	End Bytes	End Mbit/s
Frame	100.00%	265	43922	0.004	0	0	0.000
⊟ Ethernet	100.00%	265	43922	0.004	0	0	0.000
Address Resolution Protocol	12.08%	32	1920	0.000	32	1920	0.000
⊟ Internet Protocol	87.92%	233	42002	0.003	0	0	0.000
⊟ Transmission Control Protocol	85.28%	226	41122	0.003	159	15592	0.001
⊟ Hypertext Transfer Protocol	25.28%	67	25530	0.002	66	24016	0.002
Media Type	0.38%	1	1514	0.000	0	0	0.000
⊟ User Datagram Protocol	2.26%	6	810	0.000	0	0	0.000
Domain Name Service	2.26%	6	810	0.000	6	810	0.000
Internet Control Message Protocol	0.38%	1	70	0.000	1	70	0.000

Figure 5-6: The Protocol Hierarchy Statistics window shows the distribution of various protocols.

Viewing Endpoints

An *endpoint* is the place where communication ends on a particular protocol. For instance, there are two endpoints in TCP/IP communication: the IP addresses of the systems sending and receiving data, 192.168.1.5 and 192.168.0.8. An example on Layer 2 would be the communication taking place between two physical NICs and their MAC addresses. The NICs sending and receiving data have addresses of 01:00:5e:00:00:16 and 01:00:5e:01:01:06, making those addresses the endpoints of communication. You can see a graphical representation of this concept in Figure 5-7.

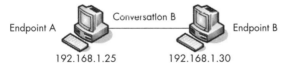

Figure 5-7: A graphical representation of endpoints on a network

When analyzing traffic, you may find that you can narrow down a problem to a specific endpoint on a network. Wireshark's Endpoints dialog (Statistics ▶ Endpoints) shows several helpful statistics for each endpoint (Figure 5-8), including the addresses of each as well as the number of packets and bytes transmitted and received by each. The tabs at the top of the window show all supported and recognized endpoints in the current capture file. Click a tab to narrow the list of endpoints to specific protocols. Check the box next to the words *Name Resolution* to use name resolution within the endpoints dialog.

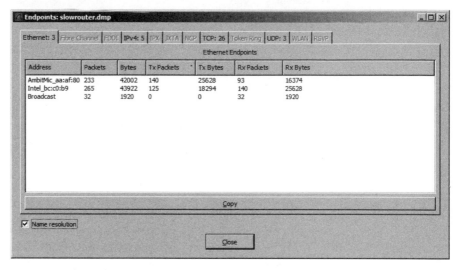

Figure 5-8: The Endpoints dialog lets you view each of the endpoints in a capture file.

You can use the Endpoints dialog to filter out specific packets for display in the Packet List pane. If you right-click a specific endpoint, you will notice several options, including the ability to create a filter to display only traffic related to this endpoint or all traffic excluding the selected endpoint. As a bonus, you can also directly export the endpoint into a colorization rule.

Conversations

A *conversation* on a network, like a conversation between two people, describes the communication that takes place between two hosts (endpoints). For example, whereas Jim and Sally's conversation might consist of "Hey, how are you?" "I'm great! Yourself?" and "Couldn't be better!" a conversation between 192.168.1.5 and 192.168.0.8 might look like "SYN," "SYN/ACK," and "ACK." (We'll look at the TCP/IP communication process in more detail in Chapter 6.)

Wireshark provides a Conversations dialog (Statistics ▸ Conversations), shown in Figure 5-9. You will see the addresses of the endpoints involved in the conversation listed as *Address A* and *Address B* as well as columns displaying the packets and bytes transmitted to and from each device.

The conversations listed in this window are divided by the protocol they use, which can be selected via the tabs at the top of the window. Right-clicking a specific conversation allows you to create filters that may be useful, such as displaying all traffic transmitted from device A, all traffic received by device B, or all traffic communicated between devices A and B.

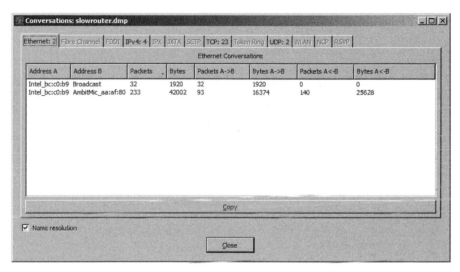

Figure 5-9: The Conversations window lets you interact with each conversation in a capture file.

The IO Graphs Window

One of the best ways to visualize trends is to view them graphically. Wireshark's IO Graphs window allows you to graph the throughput of data on a network. You might use this feature to look for spikes or lulls in the throughput of specific protocols over the course of a day on your network.

Let's look at an IO graph of an individual computer as it downloads a file from the Internet. Open the trace file FileDownload.dmp, and then select **Statistics ▸ IO Graphs**. Here you can see the low number of bytes per second early in the capture, until the graph spikes up for a brief amount of time while the file is being downloaded (Figure 5-10).

You can customize several features of this graph. The most important two things we will be modifying are the settings for the x-axis and y-axis of the graph, which allow you to modify the intervals and units used for displaying the throughput information.

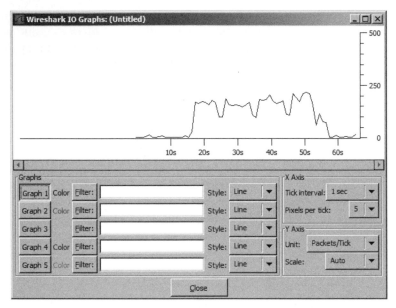

Figure 5-10: The IO graph for our capture file shows valuable trending information.

Notice that the majority of the configurable options consist of an area where you can create filters. You can create up to five unique filters (using the same syntax as a display or capture filter) and specify display colors for those filters. For instance, you could create filters to show ARP and DHCP traffic and display the lines on the graph in red and blue so that you can more easily differentiate the throughput trends between these two protocol types.

Although some of these features may seem like they would only be used in obscure situations, you will probably find yourself using them more than you might think. It is important that you familiarize yourself with these windows and options because we will be referencing them a lot in the next few chapters.

6

COMMON PROTOCOLS

This chapter is an overview of some of the more common protocols that appear in Wireshark. We will look at sample trace files containing working examples of several different protocols and then discuss how each one functions. My goal here is to help you understand each of these protocols and give you a baseline for comparison when analyzing protocols that you suspect aren't working correctly. This chapter contains some very important basic protocol information. Skipping it would be like watching part two of a movie without seeing part one—the following chapters just won't make sense.

NOTE *I won't go into great detail about the design of each individual protocol; instead, I have provided the associated RFC number for each. An RFC, or request for comments, is the official document that defines the implementation standards for protocols in the TCP/IP stack. You can search for RFC documentation at the RFC Editor home page, http://www.rfc-editor.org.*

Address Resolution Protocol

arp.pcap   We'll start with Address Resolution Protocol (ARP) because it is one of the simpler protocols, requiring only a few packets to complete its entire operation. *ARP (RFC 826)* is used to translate Layer 3 (IP) addresses into Layer 2 (MAC) addresses, thus allowing devices (such as switches and routers) to determine where other devices are located on each port.

The funny thing about ARP is that it actually provides service to two different layers of the OSI model: the network layer and the data link layer.

When a computer wants to transmit data to another computer, it must first know where that computer is. This is done with the aid of the switch or router connecting the two computers and the ARP protocol.

Now take a look at our capture file, as shown in Figure 6-1. Note that in the first packet, our source computer (01:16:ce:6e:8b:24) is sending a packet to ff:ff:ff:ff:ff:ff asking, *Who has 192.168.0.1?*.

No. ᐧ	Time	Source	Destination	Protocol	Info
213 *REF*		00:16:ce:6e:8b:24	ff:ff:ff:ff:ff:ff	ARP	who has 192.168.0.1? Tell 192.168.0.114
214	0.004081	00:13:46:0b:22:ba	00:16:ce:6e:8b:24	ARP	192.168.0.1 is at 00:13:46:0b:22:ba

Figure 6-1: The whole ARP process only involves two packets—a request and a reply.

As you learned earlier, a switch only operates on Layer 2; it has no knowledge of a computer's Layer 3 address. What does the computer do, then? Well, what do you do when you don't know the first name of the Smith you want to call? You call every Smith in the phone book until you reach the right one!

ARP provides the functionality to find the client's Layer 3 address by allowing the transmitting computer to send an *ARP broadcast*. This broadcast is a packet sent to the Layer 2 address ff:ff:ff:ff:ff:ff, the standard broadcast address; the packet is then forwarded to every computer in that switch's broadcast domain.

This packet's only function is to ask every computer it contacts whether or not it has an IP address of 192.168.0.1. Computers with a different IP address will simply drop the packet, while the one that has it will identify itself by sending a response containing its Layer 2 address back to the transmitting computer.

The second packet (also shown in Figure 6-1) shows the destination computer's ARP response to the first packet. The response is a very straightforward one: *192.168.0.1 is at 00:13:46:0b:22:ba*. From this point forward, the transmitting computer will know the Layer 2 address of the destination computer and will be able to send data directly to it.

Dynamic Host Configuration Protocol

dhcp.pcap   Dynamic Host Configuration Protocol (DHCP) is another fairly simple protocol. *DHCP (RFC 2131)* automatically provides clients with network-related configuration information, such as a domain name, NTP server address, or a unique Layer 3 (IP) address. The DHCP communication process is a client/server communication type in which the client computer requests an IP address from a DHCP server and the server acknowledges it by giving it one.

The basic functionality of DHCP is a simple four-step process. The process begins with packet 1 when the client computer sends a DHCP Discover packet to the broadcast IP address 255.255.255.255 (as shown in Figure 6-2).

No. ▾	Time	Source	Destination	Protocol	Info
1	0.000000	0.0.0.0	255.255.255.255	DHCP	DHCP Discover - Transaction ID 0x3d1d

Figure 6-2: DHCP begins with a DHCP Discover packet, as shown here.

When a client wants to obtain an IP address on a network, it must first locate a valid DHCP server on that network. It does so by sending a broadcast packet designed to locate any valid DHCP servers on the network. When a valid DHCP server receives one of these packets, it sends a response to the client in a DHCP Offer packet, as seen in packet 2 (Figure 6-3). This packet contains the IP address that the DHCP server wants to assign to the client and any other information the server is configured to supply.

No. ▾	Time	Source	Destination	Protocol	Info
2	0.000295	192.168.0.1	192.168.0.10	DHCP	DHCP Offer - Transaction ID 0x3d1d

Figure 6-3: The DHCP Offer packet is the server's response to the client.

Once the client receives this packet, it requests the addressing information from the server by sending a DHCP Request packet, which is packet 3 in our sample file. Since the client has not yet configured itself with the given IP address, this packet is once again sent as a broadcast; this tells the server that the client has accepted its offer and notifies all other DHCP servers on the network that the client is no longer accepting other offers. Once the server receives this packet, it assigns this IP address to the client and sends a DHCP ACK packet back to the client, as seen in packet 4 (Figure 6-4), signifying the end of the DHCP transaction.

No. ▾	Time	Source	Destination	Protocol	Info
1	0.000000	192.168.0.1	192.168.0.10	DHCP	DHCP ACK - Transaction ID 0x3d1e

Figure 6-4: The Packet Details pane shows all of the details for this DHCP ACK packet.

Notice that each DHCP transaction has a specific Transaction ID that can be seen under the Info heading in the Packet List pane. These *Transaction IDs* allow the DHCP server to identify and separate each client transaction. This is important because it allows you to keep each transaction separate in the analysis process.

Though we've covered only four, you may find up to eight different types of DHCP packets in a capture file. (For more on these and other DHCP functions, read the DHCP RFC.)

TCP/IP and HTTP

http.pcap TCP/IP is the basis for almost all of the communication we will discuss in this book. Because it is the most widely used network protocol, we will focus on it.

Hypertext Transfer Protocol (HTTP, RFC 2616) is the server/client–based protocol used to transfer web pages across a network. A simple HTTP transaction is a good example of TCP/IP communication. Every time you search the Internet with Google, check the weather, or even check your fantasy sports teams, you are transferring data via TCP/IP using HTTP.

TCP/IP

The TCP/IP protocol is really a stack of protocols, consisting of several different protocols on both Layers 3 and 4 of the OSI model. These protocols include TCP, IP, ARP, DHCP, ICMP, and many others.

Transmission Control Protocol (TCP, RFC 793) is a Layer 4 protocol that is commonly used because it provides an efficient method of transparent, reliable, and bi-directional communication between devices. *Bi-directional* communication means that data can be transmitted and received simultaneously from a single host.

All of the various benefits and features of TCP are made possible through different types of TCP packets and flags. In the next several paragraphs we will look at these different types of packets and what they do.

Internet Protocol (IP, RFC 791) is the Layer 3 protocol that provides the addressing system that allows communication on a network. IP is a *connectionless* protocol, which means that it requires the functionality of TCP bundled with it to ensure the reliability of transmitted data.

The traffic in the capture file begins with the establishment of a TCP/IP session, followed by the request and transmission of HTTP data and the termination of the session. Stepping through this simple communication between client and server is going to help us in understanding how TCP and IP work.

Establishing the Session

Before you can transfer data to or from another computer, the sender and receiver need to complete a TCP handshake. A *TCP handshake* is a three-step process whereby the transmitting computer (the client, in this example) establishes a connection with the destination computer (the server). You can see the handshake in the first three packets of our capture file, and it is detailed visually in Figure 6-5.

Now is a very good time to go ahead and establish our client and server computers. The client computer is shown in the first packet with IP address 145.254.160.237. The server computer is shown in the first packet with IP address 65.208.228.223.

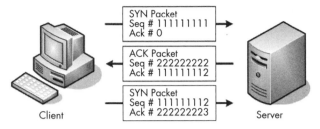

Figure 6-5: The three-step TCP handshake process

The SYN Packet

To begin the handshake process, the client sends a SYN packet to the server; this packet is designed to establish synchronization with the server, which ensures that the client and server keep their communications in the proper order. The SYN packet carries with it a 32-bit sequence number, located in the header of a TCP packet.

To view a packet's TCP information, including its sequence number, expand the TCP section under Wireshark's Packet Details pane. (You will refer to this section often because it contains a variety of useful information, including the source and destination ports used, the sequence number, the type of TCP packet, and other TCP-specific options.) Notice in the capture file that the first SYN packet's sequence number is 0, as shown in Figure 6-6.

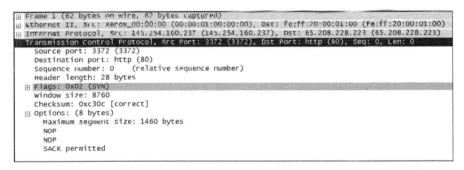

Figure 6-6: The Packet Details pane gives you all the information you need about this packet.

NOTE   *In Wireshark, TCP sequence numbers are treated as "relative" by default. Wireshark adjusts the first sequence number in a communication stream so that it is 0 rather than its true value. This is done so that the sequence numbers are easier to follow.*

SYN/ACK, the Server Response

The next step in the handshake process is the response from the server. Once the server receives the initial SYN packet from the client, it reads the packet's sequence number and uses that number in the packet it returns. The response packet is called a *SYN/ACK packet*, and it is seen in packet 2 of the example file.

The ACK portion of the packet acknowledges the SYN packet—in other words, it tells the client computer that the server received the SYN packet. It does this by incrementing the sequence number sent in the original SYN packet by one and using it as the acknowledgment number in the ACK packet. When the client receives this acknowledgment number containing the original SYN sequence number, it knows that the server can receive its communication, and vice versa. The purpose of SYN portion of the SYN/ACK is the same as in the original SYN packet: It is used to transmit a sequence number that the client system can use to acknowledge receipt.

The Final ACK Packet

Finally, the client sends an ACK packet to the server. This packet tells the server that the client received its SYN/ACK packet. As with step two of the process, the sequence number is incremented by one and sent as an acknowledgment number to the server. Once this last ACK packet is received, communication can begin.

Beginning the Flow of Data

Once the handshake has been established, all packets sent in this particular session between client and server will use sequence numbers to make sure they stay in order. However, from now on, these packets will be incremented by the size of the data frame being transmitted, rather than by one. (To learn more about how TCP packets stay organized, have a look at RFC 793.)

HTTP Request and Transmission

Once the communication session has been established, it's time for the actual request and transmission of the web page you are trying to view. This involves both HTTP and TCP.

The process begins in packet 4, our first HTTP packet, which asks the server to transmit the web page to the client. Go ahead and expand the HTTP section of this packet in the Packet Details pane to view the protocol-specific information related to this request (as shown in Figure 6-7).

```
⊟ Hypertext Transfer Protocol
  ⊟ GET /download.html HTTP/1.1\r\n
      Request Method: GET
      Request URI: /download.html
      Request Version: HTTP/1.1
  Host: www.ethereal.com\r\n
  User-Agent: Mozilla/5.0 (Windows; U; Windows NT 5.1; en-US; rv:1.6) Gecko/20040113\r\n
  Accept: text/xml,application/xml,application/xhtml+xml,text/html;q=0.9,text/plain;q=0.8,image/png,
  Accept-Language: en-us,en;q=0.5\r\n
  Accept-Encoding: gzip,deflate\r\n
  Accept-Charset: ISO-8859-1,utf-8;q=0.7,*;q=0.7\r\n
  Keep-Alive: 300\r\n
  Connection: keep-alive\r\n
  Referer: http://www.ethereal.com/development.html\r\n
  \r\n
```

Figure 6-7: The Packet Details pane shows all you would ever want to know about the request.

As you can see, this packet invokes a GET command (Request Method: GET) for the web page /download.html on the domain www.ethereal.com (Request URI: /download.html and Host: www.ethereal.com). You will also notice other information that may be useful, such as character encoding (Accept-Charset: ISO-8859-1), and the referrer location (Referrer: http://www.ethereal.com/development.html \r \n).

Once HTTP has made this initial GET request, TCP takes over the data transfer process. Throughout the rest of the capture file you will see this process repeated: HTTP will request data from the server, and the server will then use TCP to transport this data back to the client. The server lets the client know the request was valid by sending an HTTP OK message before transmitting the data. (You can see the corresponding GET and OK packets in the example file at packets 4 and 38, shown in Figure 6-8.)

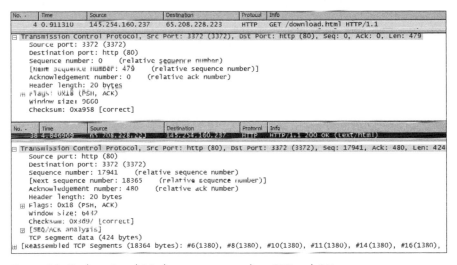

No.	Time	Source	Destination	Protocol	Info
4	0.911310	145.254.160.237	65.208.228.223	HTTP	GET /download.html HTTP/1.1

```
⊟ Transmission Control Protocol, Src Port: 3372 (3372), Dst Port: http (80), Seq: 0, Ack: 0, Len: 479
    Source port: 3372 (3372)
    Destination port: http (80)
    Sequence number: 0     (relative sequence number)
    [Next sequence number: 479    (relative sequence number)]
    Acknowledgement number: 0    (relative ack number)
    Header length: 20 bytes
 ⊞ Flags: 0x18 (PSH, ACK)
    Window size: 9660
    Checksum: 0xa958 [correct]
```

No.	Time	Source	Destination	Protocol	Info
38	4.846969	65.208.228.223	145.254.160.237	HTTP	HTTP/1.1 200 OK (text/html)

```
⊟ Transmission Control Protocol, Src Port: http (80), Dst Port: 3372 (3372), Seq: 17941, Ack: 480, Len: 424
    Source port: http (80)
    Destination port: 3372 (3372)
    Sequence number: 17941    (relative sequence number)
    [Next sequence number: 18365    (relative sequence number)]
    Acknowledgement number: 480    (relative ack number)
    Header length: 20 bytes
 ⊞ Flags: 0x18 (PSH, ACK)
    Window size: 6432
    Checksum: 0x3d97 [correct]
 ⊞ [SEQ/ACK analysis]
    TCP segment data (424 bytes)
 ⊞ [Reassembled TCP Segments (18364 bytes): #6(1380), #8(1380), #10(1380), #11(1380), #14(1380), #16(1380),
```

Figure 6-8: Packets 4 and 38 show a corresponding GET and OK.

Terminating the Session

When there is no more data to be sent over an established connection, the connection can be terminated in a manner very similar to that of the initial TCP handshake. Rather than using SYN and ACK packets however, this process uses FIN and ACK packets, as shown in Figure 6-9.

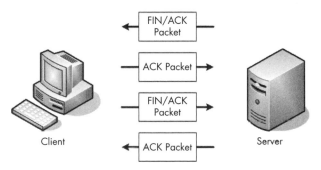

Figure 6-9: The FIN/ACK handshake process gracefully terminates a TCP connection.

When the server finishes transmitting data, it sends a FIN/ACK packet to the client, as shown in Figure 6-10. The FIN packet is designed to gracefully close a connection.

```
⊟ Transmission Control Protocol, Src Port: http (80), Dst Port: 3372 (3372), Seq: 18365, Ack: 480, Len: 0
     source port: http (80)
     Destination port: 3372 (3372)
     Sequence number: 18365     (relative sequence number)
     Acknowledgement number: 480     (relative ack number)
     Header length: 20 bytes
  ⊞ Flags: 0x11 (FIN, ACK)
     window size: 6432
     Checksum: 0x3c64 [correct]
  ⊞ [SEQ/ACK analysis]
```

Figure 6-10: You can see the details of a FIN/ACK packet in the Packet Details pane.

The client responds to the FIN packet with an ACK packet that uses the sequence numbers and incrementation rules that it finds in the FIN packet. This closes communication from the server's end of things. While the server can still receive data from the client at this point, it will no longer transmit data.

To complete the process, the client must initiate this same process again with the server. The FIN/ACK process must be initiated and acknowledged by both the client and server.

For example, in packet 40, the server sends a FIN/ACK packet to the client, and the client responds with its ACK packet in packet 41. Following that, the client sends its own FIN/ACK packet to the server, and the server closes the connection with an ACK packet, packet 43, as shown in Figure 6-11.

No.	Time	Source	Destination	Protocol	Info
40	17.905747	65.208.228.223	145.254.160.237	TCP	http > 3372 [FIN, ACK] Seq=18365 Ack=480 Win=6432 Len=0
41	17.905747	145.254.160.237	65.208.228.223	TCP	3372 > http [ACK] Seq=480 Ack=18366 Win=9236 Len=0
42	30.063228	145.254.160.237	65.208.228.223	TCP	3372 > http [FIN, ACK] Seq=480 Ack=18366 Win=9236 Len=0
43	30.393704	65.208.228.223	145.254.160.237	TCP	http > 3372 [ACK] Seq=18366 Ack=481 Win=6432 Len=0

Figure 6-11: The FIN/ACK process as seen from the Packet List pane

Domain Name System

dns.pcap   The *Domain Name System (DNS, RFC 1034)* translates one form of address into another—specifically, it translates DNS addresses, such as www.google.com or MARKETING-PC1, into their corresponding IP addresses. Some form of address translation is a requirement, since Layer 3 of the OSI model can only locate a computer if it has its IP address.

DNS translation is a very simple process, and it gets the job done in most cases using only two packets. The first packet is a request to your network's local DNS server that asks, *What is the IP address of www.google.com?* The second packet is the response from that DNS server, saying that www.google.com resides on a server with an IP address of *XX.XX.XX.XXX*.

Let's take a look at DNS in action (see Figure 6-12). Notice in the first packet of the file that a DNS packet from source 192.168.0.114 is requesting the IP address of http://www.chrissanders.org from destination 205.152.37.23. The destination IP address receives the query and responds with packet 2, which contains the IP address of the requested website, 208.113.140.24. Once this process is complete, Layer 3 can take over and complete its TCP handshake so that data transfer can begin.

No. ▴	Time	Source	Destination	Protocol	Info
1	0.000000	192.168.0.114	205.152.37.23	DNS	Standard query A chrissanders.org
2	0.112121	205.152.37.23	192.168.0.114	DNS	Standard query response A 208.113.140.24

Figure 6-12: DNS only requires two packets—a request and a response.

NOTE *As you examine the actual sample capture file, you will see several different DNS queries taking place. Often a single web page will invoke a number of queries because the information needs to be retrieved from several servers. Try creating a display filter to show only the DNS traffic and see if you can determine how many different DNS queries take place in this file.*

File Transfer Protocol

ftp.pcap The *File Transfer Protocol (FTP, RFC 959)* is a Layer 7 protocol that is used to transfer data between a server and client. Operating on ports 20 and 21, FTP is one of the most commonly used file transfer utilities. Because FTP is a client/server protocol, all communication in the capture file involves back-and-forth traffic between a client computer and a server computer. As with all TCP processes, FTP begins with a standard TCP handshake, as shown with packet 1 and in Figure 6-13 below.

No. ▴	Time	Source	Destination	Protocol	Info
1	0.000000	192.168.0.114	192.168.0.193	TCP	1137 > ftp [SYN] Seq=0 Len=0 MSS=1460
2	0.002319	192.168.0.193	192.168.0.114	TCP	ftp > 1137 [SYN, ACK] Seq=0 Ack=1 Win=16384 Len=0 MSS=1452
3	0.002338	192.168.0.114	192.168.0.193	TCP	1137 > ftp [ACK] Seq=1 Ack=1 Win=17424 Len=0

Figure 6-13: The TCP handshake is prevalent in various communication types.

Once the handshake process completes, the server sends a welcome message to the client. This message identifies the server as an FTP server and tells the client that the server is ready to accept its login credentials, as shown in Figure 6-14.

```
⊟ File Transfer Protocol (FTP)
  ⊟ 220 Chris Sanders FTP Server\r\n
      Response code: Service ready for new user (220)
      Response arg: Chris Sanders FTP Server
```

Figure 6-14: The beginning of the FTP communication process

Through the next several packets, the client sends a username (*csanders*) and a password (*echo*) to the server, and the server acknowledges them (Figure 6-15).

No. ▴	Time	Source	Destination	Protocol	Info
5	0.005259	192.168.0.114	192.168.0.193	FTP	Request: USER csanders
6	0.006560	192.168.0.193	192.168.0.114	FTP	Response: 331 Password required for csanders.
7	0.007647	192.168.0.114	192.168.0.193	FTP	Request: PASS echo
8	0.009936	192.168.0.193	192.168.0.114	FTP	Response: 230 User csanders logged in.

Figure 6-15: The username and password of the FTP user being transmitted to the server

This communication is summed up nicely in the Info column of the Packet List pane, though that window only gives a very brief summary of the packet contents. If you want to dig a little deeper, you can expand the FTP section in the Packet Details pane.

Notice that encryption is not used in our example, so the FTP password can be seen clearly in the capture file in packet 7 (Figure 6-16).

```
⊞ Frame 7 (65 bytes on wire, 65 bytes captured)
⊞ Ethernet II, Src: HonHaiPr_6e:8b:24 (00:16:ce:6e:8b:24), Dst: AsustekC_40:76:ef (00:15:f2:40:76:ef)
⊞ Internet Protocol, Src: 192.168.0.114 (192.168.0.114), Dst: 192.168.0.193 (192.168.0.193)
⊞ Transmission Control Protocol, Src Port: 1137 (1137), Dst Port: ftp (21), Seq: 16, Ack: 68, Len: 11
⊟ File Transfer Protocol (FTP)
    ⊟ PASS echo\r\n
        Request command: PASS
        Request arg: echo
```

Figure 6-16: The password of the user csanders can be seen clearly in this packet.

A connecting client uses a list of commands to interact with an FTP server. These range from viewing the contents of a directory, traversing a directory, download-ing or deleting a file, and so on. (For a complete list of the available commands visible in an FTP packet, see RFC 959.) Let's look at a few FTP commands used in our example file, beginning with packet 15, shown in Figure 6-17.

Figure 6-17: Packet 15 shows the PWD command being issued to the server.

CWD Command

As you can see, packet 15 shows a CWD command being sent from the client to the server. CWD stands for *change working directory*, and this command is invoked every time you tell an FTP client to move to a different directory on the server.

Notice in this example that the CWD command includes requests to change the working directory to /, which is the root directory of the FTP server. When you first log into an FTP server, the CWD command is issued to change to the root directory, /. Once the server receives this CWD command, it changes to the root directory and tells the client that / is now the current working directory.

SIZE Command

The next command is the SIZE command, shown in Figure 6-18. This command reports the size (in bytes) of a particular file, and it is always sent with a filename.

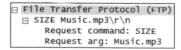

Figure 6-18: The SIZE command being sent to the server

Notice in packet 25 that the client sends the SIZE command to the server to request the size of the file Music.mp3. Packet 26 (Figure 6-19) shows the server's response, which is the file size of 4,980,924 bytes.

```
⊟ File Transfer Protocol (FTP)
  ⊟ 213 4980924\r\n
      Response code: File status (213)
      Response arg: 4980924
```

Figure 6-19: The packet returned from the issued SIZE command

RETR Command

```
⊟ File Transfer Protocol (FTP)
  ⊟ RETR Music.mp3\r\n
      Request command: RETR
      Request arg: Music.mp3
```

Figure 6-20: The RETR command is used to download a file from the FTP server.

The RETR (retrieve) command, shown in Figure 6-20, is used by the client to request the download of a file from the server. In packet 32, the client sends the RETR command to the server, requesting download of the file Music.mp3. Once the server gets this request, it begins sending the data to the client.

NOTE *The packets labeled FTP-DATA are ones containing a file that is being downloaded from or uploaded to the server.*

Telnet Protocol

telnet.pcap The *telnet protocol* (RFC 854) is an unsecured, text-based way for a server and client to communicate. It is often used to remotely administer servers, switches, routers, and other network hardware devices.

In this capture file you will see an example of a client computer (192.168.0.2) connecting to a telnet server (192.168.0.1). As you begin to step through the data being transmitted, notice that everything is sent in clear text. For this reason, the telnet protocol should not be used to transmit sensitive data.

NOTE *You can be more secure by forgoing telnet and using SSH instead.*

What type of communication is occurring in this exchange between server and client? Starting at the top, we can immediately draw several conclusions. The first several packets confirm that we are definitely seeing telnet traffic, because telnet-specific settings are being communicated between these two devices, as shown in Figure 6-21.

```
⊟ Telnet
    Command: Will Suppress Go Ahead
    Command: Do Terminal Type
    Command: Do Negotiate About Window Size
    Command: Do Terminal Speed
    Command: Do Remote Flow Control
    Command: Do Linemode
  ⊞ Suboption Begin: Linemode
    Command: Suboption End
```

Figure 6-21: The first packets of the capture file are telnet packets between server and client.

Each telnet session uses several unique options to specify communication rates and data transfer modes, which must be synchronized between client and server before communication can begin. These options account for the first 30 or so packets in the sample capture file.

The first interesting packet is number 27, which identifies the server as an OpenBSD server. Packet 29 presents a login prompt to the client, and in packet 31 you can see that the username *fake* is sent back to the server. Packet 36 requests a password from the client, which is answered in packet 38 with the password *user*, which is shown in Figure 6-22. You can now see just how insecure telnet is. This username and password combination could very well be the administrative password to one of the most important servers on your network, and it would still be shown in clear text that is readable by anyone with a packet sniffer and little bit of knowledge.

```
⊞ Frame 36 (75 bytes on wire, 75 bytes captured)
⊞ Ethernet II, Src: WesternD_9f:a0:97 (00:00:c0:9f:a0:97), Dst: Lite-OnC_3b:bf:fa (00:a0:cc:3b:bf:fa)
⊞ Internet Protocol, Src: 192.168.0.1 (192.168.0.1), Dst: 192.168.0.2 (192.168.0.2)
⊞ Transmission Control Protocol, Src Port: telnet (23), Dst Port: 1550 (1550), Seq: 143, Ack: 207, Len: 9
⊟ Telnet
     Data: Password:

⊞ Frame 38 (72 bytes on wire, 72 bytes captured)
⊞ Ethernet II, Src: Lite-OnC_3b:bf:fa (00:a0:cc:3b:bf:fa), Dst: WesternD_9f:a0:97 (00:00:c0:9f:a0:97)
⊞ Internet Protocol, Src: 192.168.0.2 (192.168.0.2), Dst: 192.168.0.1 (192.168.0.1)
⊞ Transmission Control Protocol, Src Port: 1550 (1550), Dst Port: telnet (23), Seq: 207, Ack: 152, Len: 6
⊟ Telnet
     Data: user\r\n
```

Figure 6-22: A password transmitted via telnet can be seen as clear as day.

The rest of the capture file shows the client using the established telnet session to ping several websites. You can observe this data and exactly how it is transferred by looking at the telnet section in the Packet Details pane.

MSN Messenger Service

msnms.pcap You may find that you need to analyze the traffic of an instant message conversation for several reasons. We explored one possible scenario in Chapter 5 when we suspected an employee of giving away company financial information over messenger software. There are several popular instant messaging applications, and while each one utilizes its own protocol, there are certain similarities in each. Here we'll focus specifically on traffic from the MSN Messenger Service (MSNMS). Let's see if we can't catch some employees in the act.

NOTE   *Some organizations have policies that prevent the use of messaging software, and if so, even seeing the MSNMS protocol in a capture file can set off alarms.*

The capture file begins like any TCP communication—with a simple handshake between two clients, as shown in Figure 6-23.

No. ⌄	Time	Source	Destination	Protocol	Info
1	0.000000	192.168.0.114	207.46.26.167	TCP	3331 > 1863 [SYN] Seq=0 Len=0 MSS=1460
2	0.098754	207.46.26.167	192.168.0.114	TCP	1863 > 3331 [SYN, ACK] Seq=0 Ack=1 Win=16384 Len=0 MSS=1452
3	0.098792	192.168.0.114	207.46.26.167	TCP	3331 > 1863 [ACK] Seq=1 Ack=1 Win=17424 Len=0

Figure 6-23: The TCP handshake begins the communication process.

Following this handshake, the first MSNMS packet is sent from 192.168.0.114 to a server residing outside of your local network (Figure 6-24).

No. ▾	Time	Source	Destination	Protocol	Info
4	0.098991	192.168.0.114	207.46.26.167	MSNMS	USR 93 tesla_brian@hotmail.com 1835953129.20013021.2623242

Figure 6-24: This packet shows a client inside our network communicating with a server from the outside world.

This packet is being sent from a computer on your network to a remote Microsoft server in order to establish a handshake that prepares for communication. These initial packets are marked as USR packets, as seen under the MSNMS section of the packet in the Packet Details pane. You can seen the email address of the person initiating the conversation (tesla_brian@hotmail.com) in these initial packets (Figure 6-25).

```
☐ MSN Messenger Service
      USR 93 OK tesla_brian@hotmail.com Brian\r\n
```

Figure 6-25: The user tesla_brian@hotmail.com appears to be initiating a conversation, as seen in the packet details of packet 5.

The next two packets are marked CAL packets, as shown in Figure 6-26. CAL packets are sent from the computer inside your network to an MSN server in order to establish communication with another MSNMS user.

No. ▾	Time	Source	Destination	Protocol	Info
6	0.199942	192.168.0.114	207.46.26.167	MSNMS	CAL 94 tesla_thomas@hotmail.com
7	0.300257	207.46.26.167	192.168.0.114	MSNMS	CAL 94 RINGING 1835953129

Figure 6-26: CAL packets are used here to establish communication between MSNMS users.

As you can see in packet 7, the corresponding MSNMS user has the email address *tesla_thomas@hotmail.com* (Figure 6-27).

```
⊞ Frame 6 (87 bytes on wire, 87 bytes captured)
⊞ Ethernet II, Src: HonHaiPr_6e:8b:24 (00:16:ce:6e:8b:24), Dst: D-Link_21:99:4c (00:05:5d:21:99:4c)
⊞ Internet Protocol, Src: 192.168.0.114 (192.168.0.114), Dst: 207.46.26.167 (207.46.26.167)
⊞ Transmission Control Protocol, Src Port: 3331 (3331), Dst Port: 1863 (1863), Seq: 61, Ack: 42, Len: 33
☐ MSN Messenger Service
      CAL 94 tesla_thomas@hotmail.com\r\n
```

Figure 6-27: This CAL packet lets us see the email address of the user initiating communication.

The server now acknowledges that it has received CAL packet 7 in packet 8 (Figure 6-28).

No. ▾	Time	Source	Destination	Protocol	Info
7	0.300257	207.46.26.167	192.168.0.114	MSNMS	CAL 94 RINGING 1835953129
8	0.442314	192.168.0.114	207.46.26.167	TCP	3331 > 1863 [ACK] Seq=94 Ack=69 Win=17356 Len=0

Figure 6-28: Packet 8 shows acknowledgment of packet 7.

Packet 9 is the last packet to be sent to fully establish communication. As shown in Figure 6-29, packet 9 is a JOI packet sent from the remote MSN servers, indicating that the other member of the party (tesla_thomas@ hotmail.com, in this case) has successfully joined a session and can establish communication.

No. ▴	Time	Source	Destination	Protocol	Info
9	0.510484	207.46.26.167	192.168.0.114	MSNMS	JOI tesla_thomas@hotmail.com Thomas 1616756780

Figure 6-29: Packet 9 is a JOI packet indicating that the users are now sharing a session.

The balance of the capture file contains only MSG packets, which are simply messages sent from one endpoint to another—in this case between Brian and Thomas.

The first thing that probably comes to mind when you think of this concept is, *Can I really see what they are saying?!* Well, as scary as it is, the answer is yes. Everything. By simply right-clicking one of the MSG packets and selecting **Follow TCP Stream** (as you learned to do in Chapter 5) you can see the full conversation between Brian and Thomas (Figure 6-30). This might make you be a little more careful about what you say in instant messenger conversations while on the job!

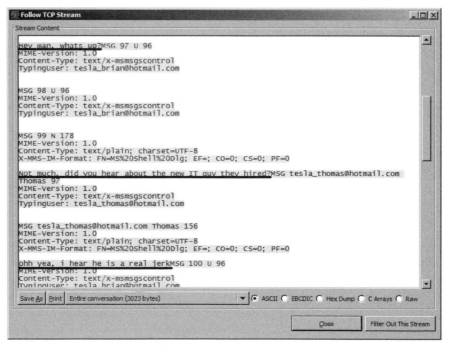

Figure 6-30: We'll see who's a jerk! You're fired!

Internet Control Message Protocol

icmp.pcap *Internet Control Message Protocol (ICMP)* is a part of the IP protocol; I like to call it a *utility protocol* because it's used for troubleshooting other protocols. If you have ever used the ping utility, you have used the ICMP protocol.

Let's see what common ICMP traffic looks like. The included capture file only contains eight packets. There are two separate pings to two separate hosts. Let's look at the packet details of packet 1, shown in Figure 6-31.

If you expand the ICMP section, you will see what little there is to an ICMP packet. The first packet is labeled as type 8, an echo (ping) request. Every ICMP packet has a numerical type associated with it, which determines how the packet is to be handled by the destination machine. (RFC 792 lists all the different types of ICMP packets.)

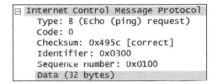

Figure 6-31: The first ping packet, packet 1

Common sense tells us that if a computer sends an echo request, it should receive an echo reply, and that's just what we see in the capture file. Packet 2 is transmitted back from the remote computer and is marked as ICMP type 0, an echo (ping) reply.

A standard ping from a Windows command line pings a host four times. You can see the ping process in the capture file and in Figure 6-32, as well. The first ping destination, 192.168.0.1, receives and replies to four pings. Following this, another ping is initiated to 72.14.207.99 (http://www.google.com), which also receives and replies to four pings.

No. ·	Time	Source	Destination	Protocol	Info
1	0.000000	192.168.0.114	192.168.0.1	ICMP	Echo (ping) request
2	0.001085	192.168.0.1	192.168.0.114	ICMP	Echo (ping) reply
3	0.996773	192.168.0.114	192.168.0.1	ICMP	Echo (ping) request
4	0.998983	192.168.0.1	192.168.0.114	ICMP	Echo (ping) reply
5	1.996801	192.168.0.114	192.168.0.1	ICMP	Echo (ping) request
6	1.999087	192.168.0.1	192.168.0.114	ICMP	Echo (ping) reply
7	2.996840	192.168.0.114	192.168.0.1	ICMP	Echo (ping) request
8	2.999177	192.168.0.1	192.168.0.114	ICMP	Echo (ping) reply

Figure 6-32: Ping, reply, ping, reply, ping, reply—you get the picture, right?

Final Thoughts

The goal of this chapter has been to introduce you to using Wireshark to analyze capture files and to use those capture files to show you how some common protocols work. Although we've only briefly covered some of the more advanced protocols, I highly recommend reading their RFCs and studying them more in depth. As the book continues on to various scenarios, we will be building on the basic concepts you've learned here.

7

BASIC CASE SCENARIOS

Now we've arrived at the real meat and bones of this book—we are ready to use Wireshark and packet analysis to actually analyze network problems.

We'll begin with a look at some simple scenarios in which our ability to analyze packets will help us to better understand what's going on behind the scenes. Then we'll look at some simple real-world troubleshooting scenarios that you could very possibly encounter on a daily basis. Let's dive in.

A Lost TCP Connection

One of the most common problems we encounter when troubleshooting is a loss of network connectivity. For now, we'll ignore the reasons why that loss of connectivity might occur and take a look at what that loss actually looks like at the packet level, so you can identify this type of problem when troubleshooting.

The small capture file tcp-con-lost.pcap (Figure 7-1) shows a loss of connectivity. The file begins with four standard TCP ACK packets sent between 10.3.71.7 and 10.3.30.1.

No. ▾	Time	Source	Destination	Protocol	Info
1	0.000000	10.3.71.7	10.3.30.1	TCP	1043 > 1048 [ACK] Seq=0 Ack=0 Win=8760 Len=0
2	0.000000	10.3.30.1	10.3.71.7	TCP	1048 > 1043 [PSH, ACK] Seq=5840 Ack=0 Win=8760 Len=648
3	0.000000	10.3.71.7	10.3.30.1	TCP	1043 > 1048 [ACK] Seq=0 Ack=2920 Win=8760 Len=0
4	0.000000	10.3.71.7	10.3.30.1	TCP	1043 > 1048 [ACK] Seq=0 Ack=5840 Win=8760 Len=0

Figure 7-1: This capture begins simply enough with a few ACK packets.

The problem begins in packet 5, where we first see TCP retransmission packets (Figure 7-2).

No. ▾	Time	Source	Destination	Protocol	Info
5	0.206000	10.3.30.1	10.3.71.7	TCP	[TCP Retransmission] 1048 > 1043 [PSH, ACK] Seq=5840 Ack=0 Win=8760 Len=648
6	0.806000	10.3.30.1	10.3.71.7	TCP	[TCP Retransmission] 1048 > 1043 [PSH, ACK] Seq=5840 Ack=0 Win=8760 Len=648
7	2.006000	10.3.30.1	10.3.71.7	TCP	[TCP Retransmission] 1048 > 1043 [PSH, ACK] Seq=5840 Ack=0 Win=8760 Len=648
8	4.406000	10.3.30.1	10.3.71.7	TCP	[TCP Retransmission] 1048 > 1043 [PSH, ACK] Seq=5840 Ack=0 Win=8760 Len=648
9	9.211000	10.3.30.1	10.3.71.7	TCP	[TCP Retransmission] 1048 > 1043 [PSH, ACK] Seq=5840 Ack=0 Win=8760 Len=648

Figure 7-2: These TCP retransmissions are a sign of a weak or dropped connection.

By design, when TCP sends a packet to a destination and does not get a reply, it waits a specified amount of time then retransmits the original packet. If a response is still not received, the source (transmitting) computer doubles the amount of time it waits for a response before sending another retransmission. The concept of a TCP retransmission is illustrated in Figure 7-3.

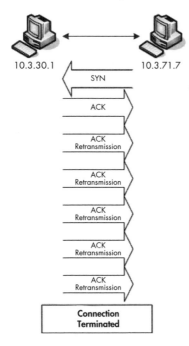

Figure 7-3: Too many TCP retransmissions are usually a sign of a connectivity problem.

As shown in Figure 7-3, the TCP retransmission process repeats until five retransmission attempts are completed, which always takes approximately 9.6 seconds under its Windows implementation. Once five retransmission attempts have failed, the connection has completely failed and the data in the transmission is lost.

If you set your Wireshark time display format to show the time that has elapsed since the previously captured packet (View ▶ Time Display Format ▶ Seconds Since Beginning of Capture), you can visualize the incrementing of time between packets (Figure 7-4).

No. ·	Time	Source	Destination	Protocol	Info
2	0.000000	10.3.30.1	10.3.71.7	TCP	1048 > 1043 [PSH, ACK] Seq=5840 Ack=0 Win=8760 Len=648
5	0.206000	10.3.30.1	10.3.71.7	TCP	[TCP Retransmission] 1048 > 1043 [PSH, ACK] Seq=5840 Ack=0 Win=8760 Len=648
6	0.600000	10.3.30.1	10.3.71.7	TCP	[TCP Retransmission] 1048 > 1043 [PSH, ACK] Seq=5840 Ack=0 Win=8760 Len=648
7	1.200000	10.3.30.1	10.3.71.7	TCP	[TCP Retransmission] 1048 > 1043 [PSH, ACK] Seq=5840 Ack=0 Win=8760 Len=648
8	2.400000	10.3.30.1	10.3.71.7	TCP	[TCP Retransmission] 1048 > 1043 [PSH, ACK] Seq=5840 Ack=0 Win=8760 Len=648
9	4.805000	10.3.30.1	10.3.71.7	TCP	[TCP Retransmission] 1048 > 1043 [PSH, ACK] Seq=5840 Ack=0 Win=8760 Len=648

Figure 7-4: Windows will retransmit up to five times by default.

Now take a closer look at the packets being retransmitted in Figure 7-4. Notice that their sequence number (Seq=5840) matches the ACK number of packet five shown at the bottom of Figure 7-1 (Ack=5840).

As you learned in Chapter 6, TCP relies on these SEQ and ACK numbers to keep a TCP stream in order. Because the SEQ number shown in the retransmission matches the ACK number of packet 5, you know that packet 5 is the packet that was lost and is now being retransmitted. The ability to locate the exact packet at which a TCP retransmission attempt begins may often lead you to clues that help you determine exactly why a loss of connectivity occurred.

Unreachable Destinations and ICMP Codes

When testing for network connectivity, one of the most commonly used tools is the ICMP ping utility. If you are lucky, the target you are pinging will respond, telling you that your ping was successful. Unfortunately, you often won't get a ping response back when you're troubleshooting; you'll receive a *Destination unreachable* message instead. Using a packet sniffer in conjunction with an ICMP utility can give you a little more information than just ICMP alone would. Let's see if we can't get inside this ICMP error message to isolate the problem.

Unreachable Destination

destunreach-
able.pcap

When you open the destunreachable.pcap file, you'll notice that the first packet in the capture file is your standard *Echo (ping) request packet* (also known as an ICMP type 8 packet) from 10.2.10.2 to 10.4.88.88, as shown in Figure 7-5.

To verify this, look at the ICMP section of the Packet Details pane—you should see this packet identified as such. Typically, though, you would want to receive an *Echo (ping) reply packet* (also known as an ICMP type 0 packet) in response to your ping.

No. ▾	Time	Source	Destination	Protocol	Info
1	0.000000	10.2.10.2	10.4.88.88	ICMP	Echo (ping) request

Figure 7-5: A standard ping request from 10.2.10.2 to 10.4.88.88

Examining packet 2 in Figure 7-6, you can see that it too is not a type 0 packet, but rather a type 3 packet, which is returned when a destination you are trying to ping is unreachable.

```
⊟ Internet Control Message Protocol
    Type: 3 (Destination unreachable)
    Code: 1 (Host unreachable)
    Checksum: 0xa7a2 [correct]
  ⊞ Internet Protocol, Src: 10.2.10.2 (10.2.10.2), Dst: 10.4.88.88 (10.4.88.88)
  ⊞ Internet Control Message Protocol
```

Figure 7-6: This ICMP type 3 packet is not what we expected.

NOTE   *If ICMP only identified the packet type, it wouldn't give us much useful information. But fortunately, it gives us a code number too, like* Code: 1 (Host unreachable). *(Several types of ICMP packets offer codes with a bit more specific information about the packet.) Notice that the source IP address in packet 2 is not the computer the ping was destined for. This is a sure sign that your echo request didn't make it to its destination.*

The listed ICMP code (1) tells us that the ping request made it to the upstream router or switch, but not to the destination host. When a host is unreachable, you will also often see an ARP broadcast sent from the router or switch. A lack of response to this ARP broadcast means that the sending device cannot find the destination device, so it sends a packet back to the source computer with an ICMP type 0, code 1 packet.

Unreachable Port

Another common task when troubleshooting is to ping a device on a specific port. This is typically done to ensure that ports that are required for certain services to run are open and accepting incoming communication.

For example, you can ensure that FTP is accessible by pinging a remote computer on port 21. If for some reason the remote computer is not accepting incoming communication on port 21, it will return an ICMP type 0, code 2 packet, which means that the destination port is unreachable.

Since you will most likely be using ICMP very often in your day-to-day network maintenance routine, you should familiarize yourself with it and some of its more common types and codes. (I keep a business card–sized quick reference in my desk; it never hurts to have something like that on hand.)

Fragmented Packets

Internet Protocol is used for the bulk of data transfer across a network, but we often overlook the fact that only so much data can fit on the wire at a time. In order to address these lower layer limitations, IP features a technology called fragmentation. *IP fragmentation* allows the protocol to break large amounts of data into chunks that can be sent across the wire and reassembled on the receiving system.

In this section, we'll look at a stream of data that has been fragmented by IP.

The trace file ipfragments.pcap consists of 24 packets that show a ping request and response. From our previous experience, we know that a typical ICMP ping-and-response sequence only takes eight packets. Then why do we have so many more here? Because in this case, each request and reply requires three packets instead of only one, so there are three times more packets than usual, as you can see in Figure 7-7.

No. ▴	Time	Source	Destination	Protocol	Info
1	0.000000	192.168.0.114	192.168.0.193	IP	Fragmented IP protocol (proto=ICMP 0x01, off=0)
2	0.000085	192.168.0.114	192.168.0.193	IP	Fragmented IP protocol (proto=ICMP 0x01, off=1480)
3	0.000094	192.168.0.114	192.168.0.193	ICMP	Echo (ping) request
4	0.004244	192.168.0.193	192.168.0.114	IP	Fragmented IP protocol (proto=ICMP 0x01, off=0)
5	0.004545	192.168.0.193	192.168.0.114	IP	Fragmented IP protocol (proto=ICMP 0x01, off=1480)
6	0.004623	192.168.0.193	192.168.0.114	ICMP	Echo (ping) reply

Figure 7-7: This ping request requires three packets rather than one because the data being transmitted is above average size.

These are the packets you would see if you were to capture a ping whose data size was larger than the default. By default, a ping only sends 32 bytes of data to its destination in Windows. However, as you can see, the ping in this trace file is transmitting 3,072 bytes of data to the client. This presents a problem because Ethernet is only designed to handle 1,500 bytes in a single packet. Therefore, IP must fragment the packets into a data stream, which is what you see in this trace file.

Determining Whether a Packet Is Fragmented

How can you tell if a packet has been fragmented? Luckily, all we need to do is look at the Packet Details pane in ipfragments.pcap. Here's how to do it:

1. In the capture file, select packet 1, and then expand the Internet Protocol section in the lower portion of the Packet Details pane.
2. You should see a section called Flags. Expand this section and you should see three fields of data, as shown in Figure 7-8. The one that is of most interest to us is the More Fragments section. Notice that for this packet, this section has a value of 1; this means that it has more fragments following it.

```
⊟ Internet Protocol, Src: 192.168.0.114 (192.168.0.114), Dst: 192.168.0.193 (192.168.0.193)
     Version: 4
     Header length: 20 bytes
  ⊞ Differentiated Services Field: 0x00 (DSCP 0x00: Default; ECN: 0x00)
     Total Length: 1500
     Identification: 0x61d1 (25041)
  ⊟ Flags: 0x02 (More Fragments)
        0... = Reserved bit: Not set
        .0.. = Don't fragment: Not set
        ..1. = More fragments: Set        ◄────────
     Fragment offset: 1480
     Time to live: 128
     Protocol: ICMP (0x01)
  ⊞ Header checksum: 0x3013 [correct]
     Source: 192.168.0.114 (192.168.0.114)
     Destination: 192.168.0.193 (192.168.0.193)
     Reassembled IP in frame: 3
  Data (1480 bytes)
```

Figure 7-8: If the More Fragments flag has a value of 1, you can expect more packets to come with it.

3. Look at the same section for packet 2; you should see that it has the same value in the More Fragments field.

4. Look at the More Fragments field for packet 3, shown in Figure 7-9. Unlike packets 1 and 2, this packet has a *0* in the More Fragments field. A value of 0 tells us that this packet is the end of the data stream and that there are no more fragments following it. The only possible values for this field are 1 and 0.

```
⊟ Internet Protocol, Src: 192.168.0.114 (192.168.0.114), Dst: 192.168.0.193 (192.168.0.193)
     Version: 4
     Header length: 20 bytes
  ⊞ Differentiated Services Field: 0x00 (DSCP 0x00: Default; ECN: 0x00)
     Total Length: 140
     Identification: 0x61d1 (25041)
  ⊟ Flags: 0x00
        0... = Reserved bit: Not set
        .0.. = Don't fragment: Not set
        ..0. = More fragments: Not set    ◄────────
     Fragment offset: 2960
     Time to live: 128
     Protocol: ICMP (0x01)
  ⊞ Header checksum: 0x54aa [correct]
     Source: 192.168.0.114 (192.168.0.114)
     Destination: 192.168.0.193 (192.168.0.193)
  ⊞ [IP Fragments (3080 bytes): #1(1480), #2(1480), #3(120)]
⊞ Internet Control Message Protocol
```

Figure 7-9: A More Fragments flag set to 0 indicates that this packet is the end of this particular data stream.

Keeping Things in Order

The next question that arises is how these fragmented packets stay in order. Since a device can receive multiple data streams at once, IP allows for an offset value so that receiving systems know the order in which to sequence fragmented packets.

To view the offset value of a fragmented packet, look under the IP section of the Packet Details pane. For example, if you view the IP section for packet 1 in the example file, you will see an offset value of 0. This tells you that this is the first packet in a series of fragmented packets.

If you browse to the second packet, you will see a dramatic change in this number (Figure 7-10): it rises to 1,480. The reason for this change is that the offset value of every fragmented packet following the first one is determined by the payload (data) size of the previous packet (minus the size of the IP header, which is 20 bytes). In the case of packet 2, this packet takes the previous offset, which is 0, and adds the size (in bytes) of the previous packet to it, which is 1,480.

```
Internet Protocol, Src: 192.168.0.114 (192.168.0.114), Dst: 192.168.0.193 (192.168.0.193)
    Version: 4
    Header length: 20 bytes
    Differentiated Services Field: 0x00 (DSCP 0x00: Default; ECN: 0x00)
    Total Length: 1500
    Identification: 0x61d1 (25041)
    Flags: 0x02 (More Fragments)
        0... = Reserved bit: Not set
        .0.. = Don't fragment: Not set
        ..1. = More fragments: Set
    Fragment offset: 1480
    Time to live: 128
    Protocol: ICMP (0x01)
    Header checksum: 0x3013 [correct]
    Source: 192.168.0.114 (192.168.0.114)
    Destination: 192.168.0.193 (192.168.0.193)
    Reassembled IP in frame: 3
Data (1480 bytes)
```

Figure 7-10: Packet 2 has an offset value based on the payload of the previous packet.

Like packet 2, packet 3 takes the previous offset of 1,480 and adds the previous packet size of 1,480, resulting in a new offset of 2,960. This concept is illustrated in Figure 7-11.

Figure 7-11: IP fragmentation breaks down large chunks of data into smaller data streams.

Take a look at examples of some other fragmented IP traffic to see if you can follow a particular data stream until it ends and keep that stream in order using each packet's offset. (This may prove to be more of a challenge than you think in a cluttered capture file.)

No Connectivity

barryscomputer .pcap and bethscomputer .pcap

Now we'll use Wireshark for the first time to analyze and troubleshoot a real-world network problem. In this scenario we have two users, Barry and Beth, who sit next to each other in an office. After a budget increase (yeah, right!), the IT department has just purchased two new computers for Barry and Beth. You are in charge of installing these new computers and making sure they are working properly. After unpacking, plugging in, and configuring both computers, you begin to test them to make sure everything is working. However, you quickly run into a problem. Barry's computer is working perfectly, but for some reason, Beth's is unable to access the Internet. Your goal is to find out why Beth's computer is unable to connect to the Internet and then fix the problem.

What We Know

The first thing you should always do when troubleshooting a problem is make a list of what you know about the issue. In this case, we know that Barry and Beth are both using identical, brand new computers. We also know that both computers have network connectivity because you assigned them IP addresses yourself and made sure that you could ping them from another computer on that network segment. Finally, we know that everything that has been configured on both computers should be exactly the same, since you configured them one after the other.

Tapping into the Wire

Once we have established what we know about the issue, it is time to devise a plan to figure out what we don't know. We begin by figuring out what type of traffic captures we need to take and where we need to place our analyzer on the network to get them.

The problem is being able to access the Internet, so the logical choice is to capture packets while Beth's computer is trying to access a website. The network Barry and Beth are connecting to is one we aren't extremely familiar with, so for the purposes of comparison, we will capture packets from Barry's computer, as well. We'll end up with two capture files: one that works and one that doesn't. Comparing the two should help us determine the problem. This process is known as *baselining*. We'll install Wireshark directly on both machines.

Analysis

Let's begin by looking at the trace file showing Barry's computer successfully accessing the Internet (barryscomputer.pcap). When you open the trace file, the first thing you will see is a textbook HTTP transaction.

As you can see in Figure 7-12, you first have an ARP broadcast looking for the Layer 2 address of the default gateway, 192.168.0.10. Once Barry's computer receives a reply to this request, it initiates a TCP handshake with the remote webserver. Once this is completed, data transfer from the server to the client begins.

No. ▴	Time	Source	Destination	Protocol	Info
1	0.000000	Microsof_2a:45:d2	Broadcast	ARP	who has 192.168.0.10? Tell 192.168.0.183
2	0.002196	D-Link_21:99:4c	Microsof_2a:45:d2	ARP	192.168.0.10 is at 00:05:5d:21:99:4c
3	0.002259	192.168.0.183	64.233.161.104	TCP	1125 > http [SYN] Seq=0 Len=0 MSS=1460
4	0.054708	64.233.161.104	192.168.0.183	TCP	http > 1125 [SYN, ACK] Seq=0 Ack=1 Win=8190 Len=0 MSS=1452
5	0.054871	192.168.0.183	64.233.161.104	TCP	1125 > http [ACK] Seq=1 Ack=1 Win=65535 Len=0
6	0.055737	192.168.0.183	64.233.161.104	HTTP	GET / HTTP/1.1
7	0.103969	64.233.161.104	192.168.0.183	TCP	http > 1125 [ACK] Seq=1 Ack=284 Win=6432 Len=0
8	0.158478	64.233.161.104	192.168.0.183	TCP	[TCP segment of a reassembled PDU]
9	0.161865	64.233.161.104	192.168.0.183	HTTP	HTTP/1.1 200 OK (text/html)

Figure 7-12: Barry's computer completes a handshake, and then HTTP data transfer begins.

Now that we know what a successful web request should look like on this network, let's take a look at the capture file from Beth's computer (bethscomputer.pcap) to see if we can find the problem. It shouldn't take too long to realize that something is definitely wrong here. As shown in Figure 7-13, the very first packet is an ARP request, not unlike the one in barryscomputer.pcap. However, this ARP request is not sent to the same IP address as the last one. Here, ARP is looking for a device with an IP address of 192.168.0.11.

No. ·	Time	Source	Destination	Protocol	Info
1	0.000000	Microsof_2a:45:d2	Broadcast	ARP	who has 192.168.0.11? Tell 192.168.0.122

Figure 7-13: Beth's computer appears to be sending an ARP request to a different IP address.

Immediately after that ARP packet, we see a bunch of NetBIOS traffic, as shown in Figure 7-14. If that other IP address wasn't a sign that something is wrong, then all of this NetBIOS traffic definitely is.

No. ·	Time	Source	Destination	Protocol	Info
2	1.271630	192.168.0.122	192.168.0.255	BROWSE	Request Announcement TESLA-MARKETING
3	2.424840	192.168.0.122	192.168.0.255	BROWSE	Host Announcement TESLA-MARKETING, Workstation, Server, NT Workstation, Potential
4	2.425448	192.168.0.122	192.168.0.255	BROWSE	Host Announcement TESLA-MARKETING, Workstation, Server, NT Workstation, Potential

Figure 7-14: All this NetBIOS traffic can't be a good thing.

NetBIOS is an older protocol that is typically only used now as a backup when TCP/IP isn't working. The appearance of NetBIOS traffic here means that since Beth's computer was unable to successfully connect to the Internet with TCP/IP, it reverted to NetBIOS as an alternate means of communication—but that also failed. (Anytime you see NetBIOS on your network, it is often a good sign that something is not quite right.)

Let's focus on the biggest anomaly we have seen so far—that is, the different IP addresses in each of the ARP packets. Barry's computer used ARP to find the location of the default gateway, 192.168.0.10. Beth's computer attempted to do the same thing; however, it tried to find the location of the IP address 192.168.0.11 and failed, as shown in Figure 7-15. The default gateway addresses are inconsistent; something is wrong.

```
Barry's Computer
⊟ Address Resolution Protocol (request)
      Hardware type: Ethernet (0x0001)
      Protocol type: IP (0x0800)
      Hardware size: 6
      Protocol size: 4
      Opcode: request (0x0001)
      Sender MAC address: 00:03:ff:2a:45:d2 (00:03:ff:2a:45:d2)
      Sender IP address: 192.168.0.183 (192.168.0.183)
      Target MAC address: 00:00:00:00:00:00 (00:00:00:00:00:00)
      Target IP address: 192.168.0.10 (192.168.0.10)


Beth's Computer
⊟ Address Resolution Protocol (request)
      Hardware type: Ethernet (0x0001)
      Protocol type: IP (0x0800)
      Hardware size: 6
      Protocol size: 4
      Opcode: request (0x0001)
      Sender MAC address: 00:03:ff:2a:45:d2 (00:03:ff:2a:45:d2)
      Sender IP address: 192.168.0.122 (192.168.0.122)
      Target MAC address: 00:00:00:00:00:00 (00:00:00:00:00:00)
      Target IP address: 192.168.0.11 (192.168.0.11)
```

Figure 7-15: The different destination addresses for each ARP packet point to a problem.

A quick check of the TCP/IP settings on both computers reveals the answer to our problem: a typo. Barry's computer is set to have a default gateway of 192.168.0.10, and Beth's computer is set to 192.168.0.11, which is the wrong address.

Summary

The errors you run into will often be due to misconfigurations. When possible, compare a machine that works properly with the one that doesn't to see if you can pinpoint the problem. In the preceding scenario we were able to pinpoint the exact packet in which things did not match up correctly. Once you can narrow down your problem, you will have a much easier time fixing it.

The Ghost in Internet Explorer

hauntedbrowser **.pcap**

This scenario begins with a disturbing call to the help desk from a user on your network named Chad. According to Chad, his computer has recently been host to a demonic possession. Despite his best efforts, the home page on his Internet browser keeps changing itself to point to various weather sites. Even if he manually changes it back to what it should be, his changes are reversed after he reboots his computer. Your goal here is to get to the bottom of this "possession" and to perform an exorcism of the ghosts that have invaded Chad's computer.

What We Know

Chad has been with our company quite a while and we know he does not have a great deal of technical expertise. In fact, he usually does more harm than good with a computer. (I don't suppose you know any users like that, do you?) From a technical standpoint, we know that Chad's computer is about two years old, runs the Windows XP operating system, and uses Internet Explorer 6 as its browser.

Tapping into the Wire

Because this problem occurs on only Chad's computer, we know that the only machine we should have to capture packets from is Chad's. Also, because it seems that Chad's home page resets every time he boots up his computer, we'll perform our capture at boot time.

In this case, we can't install Wireshark directly onto Chad's machine and capture the packets we need, so hubbing out is a good method to use. If you don't remember how this technique is administered, please refer to our discussion about it in "Hubbing Out" on page 19. The capture will start as soon as the computer is turned on and will stop as soon as it is completely booted up; no user interaction will be required.

Analysis

Although there is no user interaction with the computer during the capture, you may be a bit shocked when you open the trace file (hauntedbrowser.pcap) and see TCP and HTTP packets shooting across the wire, as shown in Figure 7-16. During a normal bootup process, you should rarely, if ever, see packets sent like this.

No.	Time	Source	Destination	Protocol	Info
1	0.000000	192.168.0.184	24.46.230.187	TCP	1038 > 1706 [SYN] Seq=0 Len=0 MSS=1460
2	0.000019	192.168.0.184	69.206.254.66	TCP	1039 > 3531 [SYN] Seq=0 Len=0 MSS=1460
3	0.001354	192.168.0.184	24.46.230.187	TCP	1038 > 1706 [SYN] Seq=0 Len=0 MSS=1460
4	0.002375	192.168.0.184	69.206.254.66	TCP	1039 > 3531 [SYN] Seq=0 Len=0 MSS=1460
5	0.338822	192.168.0.184	64.124.109.200	HTTP	GET /command/Commandv6.07.asp?Key=&t=26962 HTTP/1.1
6	0.340546	192.168.0.184	64.124.109.200	HTTP	[TCP Out-of-Order] GET /command/Commandv6.07.asp?Key=&t=26962 HTTP/1.1
7	0.638241	192.168.0.184	64.124.109.200	TCP	1040 > http [ACK] Seq=286 Ack=243 Win=65041 Len=0
8	0.638386	192.168.0.184	64.124.109.200	TCP	[TCP Dup ACK 7#1] 1040 > http [ACK] Seq=286 Ack=243 Win=65041 Len=0
9	0.800253	192.168.0.184	64.124.109.200	TCP	1040 > http [ACK] Seq=286 Ack=613 Win=64671 Len=0
10	0.800403	192.168.0.184	64.124.109.200	TCP	[TCP Dup ACK 9#1] 1040 > http [ACK] Seq=286 Ack=613 Win=64671 Len=0

Figure 7-16: Since there is no user interaction happening on Chad's computer at the time of this capture, all of these packets going across the wire should set off some alarms.

Looking more closely at these packets, we can immediately draw some conclusions. First, we know that all of these HTTP requests are being generated by Chad's computer because his IP address is listed as the source of all the TCP and HTTP packets. Also, you can see in packet 5 (Figure 7-17) that this computer is sending HTTP packets to a system on the Internet with the GET command, meaning that it is trying to download data.

```
□ Hypertext Transfer Protocol
  ⊟ GET /command/Commandv6.07.asp?Key=&t=26962 HTTP/1.1\r\n
      Request Method: GET
      Request URI: /command/Commandv6.07.asp?Key=&t=26962
      Request Version: HTTP/1.1
    User-Agent: Mozilla/3.0 (compatible; MSIE 4.0; Win32)\r\n
    Host: command.weatherbug.com\r\n
    Connection: Keep-Alive\r\n
    Cookie: wxbug_cookie=has_cookies=1; RMID=4aecf9dc45a025d0; RMFD=011H3KJTO104ym|01058k; RMFS=011H3KhLU1052U; LMB1per12h=1\r\n
    \r\n
```

Figure 7-17: Looking more closely at packet 5, we see it is trying to download data from the Internet.

Given this information, we can assume that something is running on Chad's computer at startup that shouldn't be. A look further down the Packet List pane provides us with an insight that may just be the root of our problem. Packets 11 and 12 do a DNS request for a server on the weatherbug.com domain, as shown in Figure 7-18.

No.	Time	Source	Destination	Protocol	Info
11	3.725242	192.168.0.184	205.152.37.23	DNS	Standard query A deskwx.weatherbug.com
12	3.734060	192.168.0.184	205.152.37.23	DNS	Standard query A deskwx.weatherbug.com

Figure 7-18: A DNS query to the weatherbug.com domain gives a clue to the culprit.

Considering Chad's home page keeps changing to weather sites when he boots up, we have probably just found our culprit. Upon further investigation of Chad's computer, our assumptions prove correct, and we find that the computer has the WeatherBug desktop program running in the background, set to download new weather information and display it on the home page after every restart. After uninstalling this software, the problem ceases.

Summary

You will find that many computer and network problems are not the fault of a particular computer or network, but rather the software running on it. In this scenario, a weather-tracking program had been installed on Chad's computer, causing him to think it was "possessed" because his web browser's home page changed after every restart. By capturing and examining packets with Wireshark, we were able to uncover this program running silently in the background.

Examining problems at the packet level makes troubleshooting much easier because so little is hidden.

Inbound FTP

ftpclientdenied
.pcap and
ftpserverdenied
.pcap

In this next scenario, let's imagine you have just set up a new FTP server for your company. Clients will be connecting to this FTP server both internally and externally to download and upload large amounts of data. You have set up the FTP server software and have created a generic username and password for use by all employees. However, for some reason when you're trying to test the server from a remote machine, you are unable to access it through FTP client software.

What We Know

We know that this server is brand new and has just been set up using Windows Server 2003, with all of the latest updates and service packs installed. We have verified that the FTP software is set up correctly and is active. We have also verified that the client trying to connect to the FTP server is using the appropriate IP address and login credentials.

Tapping into the Wire

Because this problem involves both a server and a client machine, we will take a capture file from both computers. The capture from the client will be done when the FTP client software tries to connect to the server. The capture from the server will be done at the moment the client is trying to connecting to the FTP software. By capturing the files in this fashion, we will be able to determine whether the problem originates with the client or the server; then we can proceed with further investigation. We'll install Wireshark directly on these two machines for the purpose of these captures.

Analysis

Let's start with the client to make sure it is initiating communication as it should be. Looking at the capture file ftpclientdenied.pcap (Figure 7-19), we see that it is doing exactly what it should be doing. It begins the TCP hand-shake process by issuing a SYN packet to the remote server, 192.168.0.182. However, the server does not respond, so the client issues two more SYN packets to try and establish communication.

No. ▾	Time	Source	Destination	Protocol	Info
1	0.000000	192.168.0.193	192.168.0.182	TCP	1596 > ftp [SYN] Seq=0 Len=0 MSS=1460
2	2.944417	192.168.0.193	192.168.0.182	TCP	1596 > ftp [SYN] Seq=0 Len=0 MSS=1460
3	8.979791	192.168.0.193	192.168.0.182	TCP	1596 > ftp [SYN] Seq=0 Len=0 MSS=1460

Figure 7-19: The client tries to establish connection with SYN packets but gets no response; then it sends a few more.

This process continues for about nine seconds before the client determines it is unable to connect to the server. The client is doing exactly what it is supposed to do concerning the initiation of the TCP handshake, so it is safe to assume the problem most likely does not reside with the client.

Now let's look at the trace from the server's point of view in the ftpserverdenied.pcap capture file. The two capture files look amazingly similar; in fact, the only difference between the two files is that the source and destination addresses on the SYN packets have been switched around (Figure 7-20). This tells us that the packets being sent from the client are indeed making it to the server, but that for some unknown reason, the server is not accepting them.

Client

No. ▾	Time	Source	Destination	Protocol	Info
1	0.000000	192.168.0.193	192.168.0.182	TCP	1596 > ftp [SYN] Seq=0 Len=0 MSS=1460
2	2.944417	192.168.0.193	192.168.0.182	TCP	1596 > ftp [SYN] Seq=0 Len=0 MSS=1460
3	6.035374	192.168.0.193	192.168.0.182	TCP	1596 > ftp [SYN] Seq=0 Len=0 MSS=1460

Server

No. ▾	Time	Source	Destination	Protocol	Info
1	0.000000	192.168.0.193	192.168.0.182	TCP	1637 > ftp [SYN] Seq=0 Len=0 MSS=1460
2	2.992575	192.168.0.193	192.168.0.182	TCP	1637 > ftp [SYN] Seq=0 Len=0 MSS=1460
3	6.035158	192.168.0.193	192.168.0.182	TCP	1637 > ftp [SYN] Seq=0 Len=0 MSS=1460

Figure 7-20: The client and server trace files are almost identical.

There are typically three main reasons a computer will reject packets sent to it.

- The service that is supposed to be accepting those packets is not running. Because we know that the FTP server software is running and ready to accept connections, this can't be our problem.

- The server is experiencing a very high amount of traffic. In these situations the server's buffer can become filled so that it is unable to communicate at all with some clients. Once again, this can't be the cause of our problem, because the server has just been set up and is under no load whatsoever.

- The packets are being intentionally blocked. What would intentionally block packets from being received by a computer? Something that is doing exactly what it is supposed to! After closer examination of the server, we find that the Windows firewall is enabled on it and is blocking all incoming traffic on FTP ports.

Summary

Packet analysis won't always point you straight to your problem. In fact, in this scenario nothing specific in the captures identified the firewall as the problem. However, this analysis allowed us to narrow down the problem specifically to the server.

Sometimes you must troubleshoot problems that affect dozens or even hundreds of systems. If you can use packet analysis in those situations to narrow down your problem to a specific computer, then you have saved yourself a tremendous amount of time.

It's Not My Fault!

http-fault-post
.pcap

Some network users are absolutely impossible. Have you ever had a user who always blames the IT department for every little problem he or she has? Erin is exactly that kind of user. Any time the network is running the least bit below an optimal state, she is always glad to let you know.

In this particular scenario, Erin is trying to submit an online order for a manufacturing-related product. The problem is that when she submits the form to order the product, it returns an HTTP 403 (Forbidden) error. We know that this error is almost always caused by a problem on the remote website, but Erin has complained enough that your boss has asked you to prove to her that this is truly the case. We have to show that this problem is due to the remote server, not something at the packet level.

What We Know

We know that Erin has never been able to successfully send data through the web form in question, but she can submit any other web form she needs to without a hitch. Looking at the source code of the website in question, we see that it is using a standard HTML form with nothing flashy attached to it.

Tapping into the Wire

Installing Wireshark on Erin's computer is the easiest way to get the capture file we need. Once it's installed, we can begin the capture process and Erin can then attempt to fill out and submit her form, at which point we will begin the analysis process.

Analysis

The trace file (http-fault-post.pcap) begins with a standard TCP handshake between Erin's computer, 24.4.97.251, and the remote webserver, 216.23.168.114, as shown in Figure 7-21.

No. ▾	Time	Source	Destination	Protocol	Info
1	0.000000	24.4.97.251	216.23.168.114	TCP	2580 > http [SYN] Seq=0 Len=0 MSS=1460
2	0.027956	216.23.168.114	24.4.97.251	TCP	http > 2579 [SYN, ACK] Seq=0 Ack=0 Win=16384 Len=0 MSS=1460
3	0.028045	24.4.97.251	216.23.168.114	TCP	2579 > http [ACK] Seq=0 Ack=1 Win=65535 Len=0

Figure 7-21: So far, so good. A standard TCP handshake begins communication with Erin's computer and the remote webserver.

Shortly thereafter, HTTP communication begins between the client and server. Notice in the Info column (Figure 7-22) that it doesn't take too long before the client receives the HTTP 403 message from the server, which is the source of the complaint.

No. ▾	Time	Source	Destination	Protocol	Info
9	0.065496	216.23.168.114	24.4.97.251	HTTP	HTTP/1.1 403 Forbidden (text/html)

Figure 7-22: The HTTP 403 message comes pretty quickly.

The 403 error happens in packet 9. Because this is really the only stream of data in the capture we are concerned with, right-click it and choose **Follow TCP Stream** to view the clear text reassembly of the HTTP transaction, as shown in Figure 7-23.

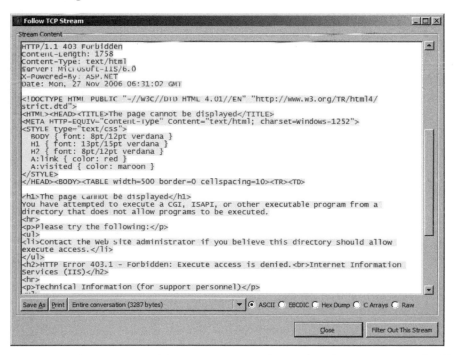

Figure 7-23: The TCP stream of the HTTP transaction that results in the 403 message should be all the proof you need.

Looking at this TCP stream, we first see the form data being sent from our client to the server. At this point we should see a response from the server with something saying the data from the form was accepted, but instead we see the 403 response. This is enough to prove that the problem lies with the remote server and not on your network.

Summary

Packet analysis is often a great tool to use when you must prove that you actually do know what you're doing. Not only do you sometimes have to prove your assumptions to management, but sometimes you have to prove them to yourself.

In this case, the plaintext interpretation of the TCP stream can be shown to your supervisor to put an end to Erin's tirade against the IT department.

An Evil Program

evilprogram
.pcap

This scenario is much like the situation with Chad's haunted computer. In this case, however, we have a little bit more going on. Mandy is another user on our network who is complaining about strange things happening in her browser. The browser keeps changing its home page to a faux security website at random times throughout the day. Not only that, she is seeing quite a few pop-ups and her computer is generally sluggish.

If you have any computer repair experience, you are probably pretty sure this is a spyware problem—and you are right. However, rather than just running a spyware-removal tool, we are going to take a trace of the computer so we can see exactly what this spyware is doing to give Mandy's computer so much trouble.

What We Know

We don't need to know a whole lot to solve this particular problem. We know that Mandy's computer is operating very slowly and that her browser is being hijacked constantly. Her computer is running virus-scanning software, so viruses shouldn't be too much of a concern for us.

Tapping into the Wire

When troubleshooting a spyware-related problem, it is always a good idea to begin your trace file when the computer boots up. Most spyware applications tend to "phone home" to check for updates and such when an infected computer starts up.

We'll begin our capture file as soon as the computer boots up and continue capturing packets until a minute or so after the startup process has completed. In this case, hubbing out or ARP cache poisoning are the best methods to use for intercepting this machine's packets. Since there is a lot of traffic flowing on our network, we'll create the capture file using a capture filter that only catches traffic to and from Mandy's computer.

Analysis

This is a pretty big capture file, so we'll start at the beginning. The first two packets (shown in Figure 7-24) are pretty common sights when a computer starts up and begins to initialize its TCP/IP stack.

No. ▲	Time	Source	Destination	Protocol	Info
1	0.000000	0.0.0.0	255.255.255.255	DHCP	DHCP Request - Transaction ID 0x9a71fd19
2	0.210908	Intel_b7:f2:f5	Broadcast	ARP	who has 24.6.125.19? Gratuitous ARP

Figure 7-24: The first two packets show Mandy's computer getting its IP address and making sure there are no IP conflicts.

The first packet shows the computer asking the DHCP server for its IP lease. Typically, there is a response to this packet from the DHCP server, but since this is a broadcast packet, our capture filter doesn't allow it to be shown.

The second packet is an ARP packet that we call a gratuitous ARP. A *gratuitous ARP* is an ARP broadcast-type packet that is used to ensure that no other machine on the network has the same IP address as the sending machine. You should only see gratuitous ARP requests going out; if you see a gratuitous ARP reply, that means another computer on the network has your IP address. In this capture we only see requests, so we are in good shape.

The third packet in the capture is one we should be concerned about. At this point in the computer's startup process, TCP/IP has yet to fully initialize: You can see that it is still sending out its gratuitous ARP packets, as shown in Figure 7-25. But packet 3 shows that a device outside our network is attempting to communicate with Mandy's computer on port 5554.

No. ▲	Time	Source	Destination	Protocol	Info
1	0.000000	0.0.0.0	255.255.255.255	DHCP	DHCP Request - Transaction ID 0x9a71fd19
2	0.210908	Intel_b7:f2:f5	Broadcast	ARP	who has 24.6.125.19? Gratuitous ARP
3	0.727104	67.70.67.186	24.6.125.19	TCP	2431 > 5554 [SYN] Seq=0 Len=0 MSS=1440
4	0.020358	Intel_b7:f2:f5	Broadcast	ARP	who has 24.6.125.19? Gratuitous ARP
5	0.796948	67.70.67.186	24.6.125.19	TCP	2860 > 9898 [SYN] Seq=0 Len=0 MSS=1440
6	0.204513	Intel_b7:f2:f5	Broadcast	ARP	who has 24.6.125.19? Gratuitous ARP

Figure 7-25: Packets 3 and 5 come far too early for the client to be able to receive them.

At this point in the initialization process, no machines should be trying to communicate with Mandy's computer, since it isn't even ready to accept communication yet. Therefore, Mandy's computer simply drops the packet and goes on with its startup process. Another packet like this appears in packet 5 of the capture file, however this time, the packet has changed the ports it is using and tries to connect to port 9898, as shown in Figure 7-26. Very tricky.

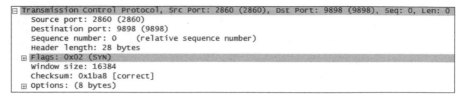

```
⊟ Transmission Control Protocol, Src Port: 2860 (2860), Dst Port: 9898 (9898), Seq: 0, Len: 0
    Source port: 2860 (2860)
    Destination port: 9898 (9898)
    Sequence number: 0     (relative sequence number)
    Header length: 28 bytes
  ⊞ Flags: 0x02 (SYN)
    Window size: 16384
    Checksum: 0x1ba8 [correct]
  ⊞ Options: (8 bytes)
```

Figure 7-26: Another remote connection attempt is made before Mandy's computer is ready for it.

Once again, Mandy's computer is not ready for communication and simply drops the packet.

Once Mandy's computer is ready to finally accept communication, it receives another one of these packets at packet 10. Mandy does not have any services running on the requested port that can accept the TCP handshake, so her computer replies to the remote computer with a TCP RST packet, terminating the communication, as shown in Figure 7-27.

No. ▾	Time	Source	Destination	Protocol	Info
10	556.468939	203.101.42.68	24.6.125.19	TCP	1560 > 4899 [SYN] Seq=0 Len=0 MSS=1460
12	556.478580	24.6.125.19	203.101.42.68	TCP	4899 > 1560 [RST, ACK] Seq=0 Ack=1 Win=0 Len=0
14	557.229229	203.101.42.68	24.6.125.19	TCP	1560 > 4899 [SYN] Seq=0 Len=0 MSS=1460
15	557.229235	24.6.125.19	203.101.42.68	TCP	4899 > 1560 [RST, ACK] Seq=0 Ack=1 Win=0 Len=0
16	557.932751	203.101.42.68	24.6.125.19	TCP	1560 > 4899 [SYN] Seq=0 Len=0 MSS=1460
17	557.932857	24.6.125.19	203.101.42.68	TCP	4899 > 1560 [RST, ACK] Seq=0 Ack=1 Win=0 Len=0

Figure 7-27: Another connection attempt is made, and this time Mandy's computer is ready for it; however, it doesn't have a use for the connection, so it simply sends a RST packet to end the connection.

This process repeats throughout the next several series of packets. Mandy's computer is doing exactly what it is supposed to be doing by refusing this communication.

Filtering out the Good

If you continue to scroll down to packet 68, you will see the first legitimate communication, as shown in Figure 7-28.

No. ▾	Time	Source	Destination	Protocol	Info
68	1132.623271	24.6.125.19	216.148.227.68	DNS	Standard query A updatekeepalive.mcafee.com
69	1132.658710	216.148.227.68	24.6.125.19	DNS	Standard query response A 216.49.88.118

Figure 7-28: This packet shows the beginning of the process of updating virus-scanning software.

Here Mandy's computer begins to communicate with its virus-scanning software and downloads an update. These packets are valid, and since we are only looking for suspicious packets, we'll filter these out by filtering all traffic to or from the McAfee IP address shown in packet 68 (Figure 7-29).

NOTE   *Hopefully you remember how to create filters from our previous discussion. The filter you want to create to hide any traffic to or from the McAfee server is* `!ip.addr==216.49.88.118`*.*

Figure 7-29: This filter removes all of the legitimate traffic so we can focus on what is abnormal.

Remote Connection Attempts

Once you have this filter set up, the next packet of interest is packet 147, shown in Figure 7-30.

No. ▴	Time	Source	Destination	Protocol	Info
147	1202.816709	221.143.42.254	24.6.125.19	Messen	NetrSendMessage request

Figure 7-30: Packet 147 is a messenger packet. We need to investigate this further.

This is a messenger packet being sent from a device on the Internet. You can view the payload of the messenger packet by viewing the packet's Packet Bytes pane, as shown in Figure 7-31.

```
00b0  00 00 d2 00 00 00 00 00   00 00 d2 00 00 00 41 4c   ........ ......AL
00c0  45 52 54 3a 20 44 41 4e   47 45 52 4f 55 53 20 53   ERT: DAN GEROUS S
00d0  50 59 57 41 52 45 20 56   49 52 55 53 20 46 4f 55   PYWARE V IRUS FOU
00e0  4e 44 0a 44 45 4c 45 54   45 20 54 48 49 53 20 53   ND.DELET E THIS S
00f0  50 59 57 41 52 45 20 56   49 52 55 53 20 49 4d 4d   PYWARE V IRUS IMM
0100  45 44 49 41 54 45 4c 59   0a 56 49 53 49 54 20 54   EDIATELY .VISIT T
0110  48 45 20 57 45 42 53 49   54 45 20 57 57 57 2e 50   HE WEBSI TE WWW.P
0120  34 55 32 2e 43 4f 4d 20   54 4f 20 43 4f 4e 54 49   4U2.COM  TO CONTI
0130  4e 55 45 0a 0a 4e 4f 54   45 3a 20 44 49 53 41 42   NUE..NOT E: DISAB
0140  4c 49 4e 47 20 59 4f 55   52 20 22 4d 45 53 53 45   LING YOU R "MESSE
0150  4e 47 45 52 22 20 41 4e   44 20 22 41 4c 45 52 54   NGER" AN D "ALERT
0160  45 52 22 20 57 49 4c 4c   4f 57 53 20 53 45 52 56   ER" WIND OWS SERV
0170  49 43 45 20 57 49 4c 4c   20 42 4c 4f 43 4b 20 54   ICE WILL  BLOCK T
0180  48 45 53 45 20 4d 45 53   53 41 47 45 53 0a 0a 00   HESE MES SAGES...
```

Figure 7-31: The payload of packet 147

Thankfully, the messenger service is disabled on our network, so Mandy never sees this message. You can verify that this message is never delivered by seeing the ICMP Destination unreachable packet our computer sends to the remote computer directly following the initial connection attempt, as shown in Figure 7-32.

No. ▴	Time	Source	Destination	Protocol	Info
147	1202.816709	221.143.42.254	24.6.125.19	Messen	NetrSendMessage request
148	1202.816878	24.6.125.19	221.143.42.254	ICMP	Destination unreachable (Port unreachable)

Figure 7-32: The computer never receives the messenger packet because the service is disabled.

At packet 210 (Figure 7-33), we begin to see something very troubling.

No. ▴	Time	Source	Destination	Protocol	Info
210	1617.530663	24.136.28.59	24.6.125.19	TCP	3092 > 1025 [SYN] Seq=0 Len=0 MSS=1460
211	1617.530814	24.6.125.19	24.136.28.59	TCP	1025 > 3092 [SYN, ACK] Seq=0 Ack=1 Win=17520 Len=0 MSS=1460
212	1617.534487	24.136.28.59	24.6.125.19	TCP	3095 > 1025 [SYN] Seq=0 Len=0 MSS=1460
213	1617.534608	24.6.125.19	24.136.28.59	TCP	1025 > 3095 [SYN, ACK] Seq=0 Ack=1 Win=17520 Len=0 MSS=1460
214	1617.598282	24.136.28.59	24.6.125.19	TCP	3099 > 3127 [SYN] Seq=0 Len=0 MSS=1460

Figure 7-33: There is another remote connection attempt, but this time Mandy's computer actually responds.

Just like before, we have a remote computer trying to establish communication with Mandy's computer by initiating a TCP handshake. However, unlike before, her computer actually responds this time, via port 1025. This means that there is a service running on this port that is listening for a connection from the outside. This is *never* a good thing!

Closing In on the Problem

At this point you can scroll down for a while and continue to see a lot of the same thing. Various connection attempts are made to Mandy's computer, some of which are successful and some of which are not. Regardless, until now those connection attempts have not really resulted in much of interest to us—that is, until packet number 357, shown in Figure 7-34.

No.	Time	Source	Destination	Protocol	Info
357	9901.421104	24.191.223.102	24.6.125.19	DCERPC	Bind: call_id: 127 ISystemActivator V0.0
358	9901.421594	24.6.125.19	24.191.223.102	DCERPC	Bind_ack: call_id: 127 Provider rejection, reason: Abstract syntax not supported
360	9901.535034	24.191.223.102	24.6.125.19	ISyste	RemoteCreateInstance request
362	9901.535280	24.6.125.19	24.191.223.102	DCERPC	Fault: call_id: 229 ctx_id: 0 status: nca_unk_if

Figure 7-34: Packet 357 is a DCEPRC packet initiated by a host outside of our network.

Packet 357 is a DCEPRC, or a Remote Procedure Call (RPC) packet. *RPC* is a protocol used to remotely execute programs on a system. Let's see—here we have a computer outside of our network trying to remotely start a program on a computer inside our network. It doesn't take a PhD in computer science to figure out that this should not be happening.

Now we will want to watch Mandy's computer very closely to see exactly what it communicates back to this remote system. As you monitor its communication, you will eventually get to packet 381, in which our client makes a DNS request for updates.virtumonde.com, as shown in Figure 7-35.

No.	Time	Source	Destination	Protocol	Info
381	11477.76286	24.6.125.19	216.148.227.68	DNS	Standard query A updates.virtumonde.com
382	11477.83280	216.148.227.68	24.6.125.19	DNS	Standard query response A 208.48.15.13 A 208.48.15.11

Figure 7-35: At this point, Mandy's computer makes a DNS request to a remote update server.

If something like this happens and you aren't familiar with the website being queried, do an Internet search. If you search for the keyword *virtumonde*, you will find a lot of results relating to spyware and server hosting.

Let's take a closer look at the communication between Mandy's computer and the remote virtumonde server. To do so, open the Conversations window and filter out all traffic between our host, 24.6.125.19, and the virtumonde server, 208.48.15.13 (see Figure 7-36). Once you do this, you'll have only a few packets to look at, which will makes things a lot easier.

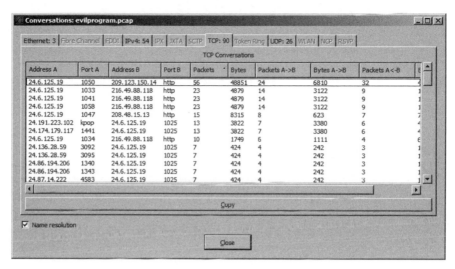

Figure 7-36: The Conversations window allows us to focus on only these two endpoints.

Continuing down the list of packets, we see in packet 386 that our client goes out to the virtumonde server and requests the download of a file called bkinst.exe (Figure 7-37).

```
⊟ Hypertext Transfer Protocol
  ⊟ GET /bkinst.exe HTTP/1.1\r\n
      Request Method: GET
      Request URI: /bkinst.exe
      Request Version: HTTP/1.1
    User-Agent: Mozilla/4.0 (compatible; MSIE 6.0; Windows NT 5.1)\r\n
    Host: updates.virtumonde.com\r\n
    Cache-Control: no-cache\r\n
    \r\n
```

Figure 7-37: Mandy's computer requests to download a file from the virtumonde server in this packet.

If you do an Internet search for this file, you will see that it is associated with spyware, browser hijacking, and pretty much every other bad thing you can think of. You have successfully found the problem affecting Mandy's computer.

Summary

In this scenario we learned that the reason Mandy's computer was doing strange things was related to a spyware application that was being downloaded to her computer via a background RPC service. But what was the point of going through all of that just to find out something we already knew?

We went through this analysis process so that we could better understand what was happening on the network. If Mandy's computer was able to be infected with this spyware, chances are it could happen to somebody else, as well. Learning the ports and services used in this communication process will allow us to block them at the firewall level to prevent problems in the future. Even if a problem may seem like it has a very simple fix, going the extra mile to find out exactly *why* it is happening can be very useful in the future.

Final Thoughts

The scenarios provided in this chapter are very simple, but they are also very important in helping you familiarize yourself with Wireshark, packet analysis, and network troubleshooting in general. The rest of the book will be written in much the same format but will focus on different areas of real-world packet analysis.

8

FIGHTING A SLOW NETWORK

As a network administrator, much of your time will be spent fixing computers and services that are running more slowly than they should be. The most common complaint heard by IT staff is that the network is slow. However, just because someone says that the network is running slowly does not mean that a network problem is to blame.

Therefore, before you begin to tackle a slow network problem, you first have to determine whether the network is, in fact, running slowly. In this chapter we will look at several different scenarios in which a user is complaining that the network is slow.

Anatomy of a Slow Download

slowdownload .pcap

Let's take a look at the anatomy of a slow download at the packet level.

Scrolling through all of the packets (as shown in Figure 8-1), you will see a lot of standard HTTP and TCP traffic, and this shows the download taking place. As we learned in our discussion of HTTP in Chapter 6, HTTP is used to request the data from a webserver, and then TCP is used to download that data from the remote server.

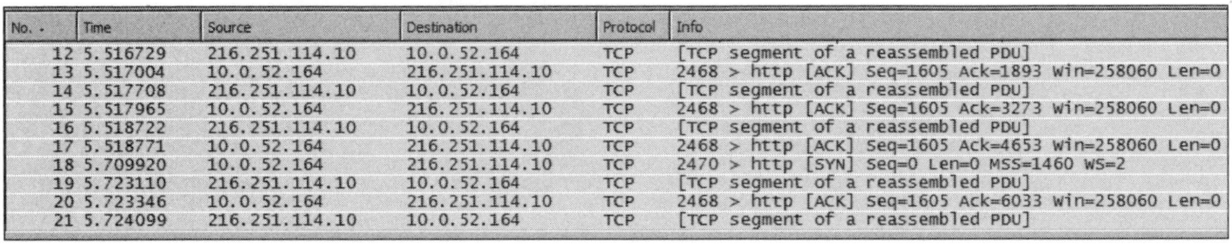

No. | Time | Source | Destination | Protocol | Info
12 5.516729 216.251.114.10 10.0.52.164 TCP [TCP segment of a reassembled PDU]
13 5.517004 10.0.52.164 216.251.114.10 TCP 2468 > http [ACK] Seq=1605 Ack=1893 Win=258060 Len=0
14 5.517708 216.251.114.10 10.0.52.164 TCP [TCP segment of a reassembled PDU]
15 5.517965 10.0.52.164 216.251.114.10 TCP 2468 > http [ACK] Seq=1605 Ack=3273 Win=258060 Len=0
16 5.518722 216.251.114.10 10.0.52.164 TCP [TCP segment of a reassembled PDU]
17 5.518771 10.0.52.164 216.251.114.10 TCP 2468 > http [ACK] Seq=1605 Ack=4653 Win=258060 Len=0
18 5.709920 10.0.52.164 216.251.114.10 TCP 2470 > http [SYN] Seq=0 Len=0 MSS=1460 WS=2
19 5.723110 216.251.114.10 10.0.52.164 TCP [TCP segment of a reassembled PDU]
20 5.723346 10.0.52.164 216.251.114.10 TCP 2468 > http [ACK] Seq=1605 Ack=6033 Win=258060 Len=0
21 5.724099 216.251.114.10 10.0.52.164 TCP [TCP segment of a reassembled PDU]

Figure 8-1: We need to filter out all of this HTTP and TCP traffic.

In order to filter out the abnormal traffic that is slowing our download, we'll use the Expert Infos window. To open this window, click **Analyze** in the menu bar and select **Expert Infos**. You should see something like Figure 8-2.

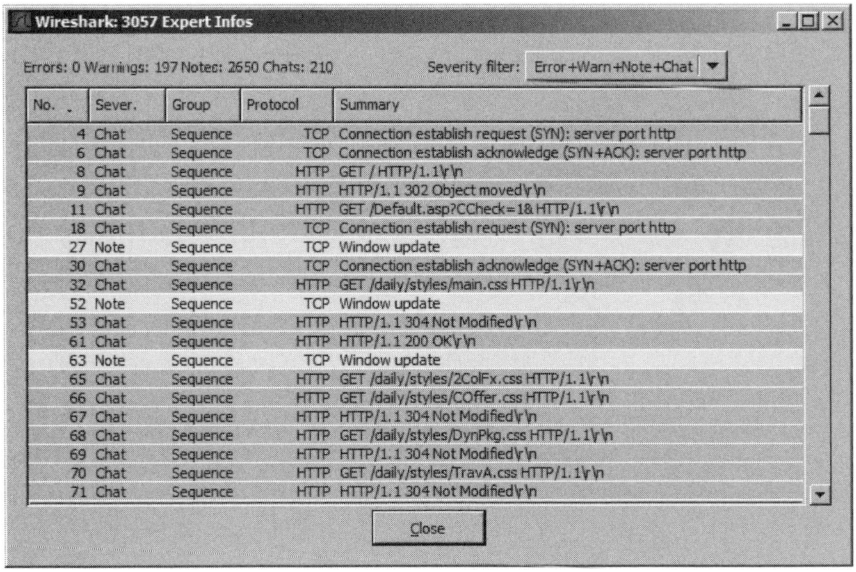

Wireshark: 3057 Expert Infos
Errors: 0 Warnings: 197 Notes: 2650 Chats: 210
Severity filter: Error+Warn+Note+Chat
No. | Sever. | Group | Protocol | Summary
4 Chat Sequence TCP Connection establish request (SYN): server port http
6 Chat Sequence TCP Connection establish acknowledge (SYN+ACK): server port http
8 Chat Sequence HTTP GET / HTTP/1.1\r\n
9 Chat Sequence HTTP HTTP/1.1 302 Object moved\r\n
11 Chat Sequence HTTP GET /Default.asp?CCheck=1& HTTP/1.1\r\n
18 Chat Sequence TCP Connection establish request (SYN): server port http
27 Note Sequence TCP Window update
30 Chat Sequence TCP Connection establish acknowledge (SYN+ACK): server port http
32 Chat Sequence HTTP GET /daily/styles/main.css HTTP/1.1\r\n
52 Note Sequence TCP Window update
53 Chat Sequence HTTP HTTP/1.1 304 Not Modified\r\n
61 Chat Sequence HTTP HTTP/1.1 200 OK\r\n
63 Note Sequence TCP Window update
65 Chat Sequence HTTP GET /daily/styles/2ColFx.css HTTP/1.1\r\n
66 Chat Sequence HTTP GET /daily/styles/COffer.css HTTP/1.1\r\n
67 Chat Sequence HTTP HTTP/1.1 304 Not Modified\r\n
68 Chat Sequence HTTP GET /daily/styles/DynPkg.css HTTP/1.1\r\n
69 Chat Sequence HTTP HTTP/1.1 304 Not Modified\r\n
70 Chat Sequence HTTP GET /daily/styles/TravA.css HTTP/1.1\r\n
71 Chat Sequence HTTP HTTP/1.1 304 Not Modified\r\n
Close

Figure 8-2: The Expert Infos window shows us chats, warnings, errors, and notes.

By default, the Expert Infos window shows all warning, error, note, and chat traffic from our capture file. Since chat traffic is not usually suspect (at least for this purpose), we'll modify the default setting by selecting **Error+Warn+Note** from the drop-down box next to the words *Severity filter*. Our new Expert Infos window will look like Figure 8-3.

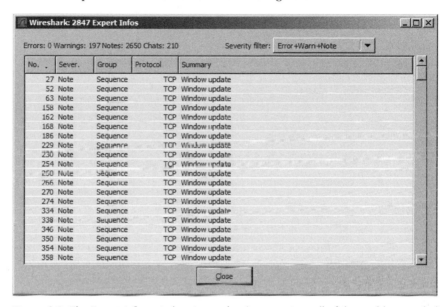

Figure 8-3: The Expert Infos window (sans chats) summarizes all of the problems with this download.

Notice in Figure 8-3 that an abundance of the packets in our capture file are *TCP Window update packets*. The transmission rate of data over a network is determined by the size of the TCP receive window. When clients are transferring data, they will constantly send TCP Window update packets to each other as their ability to receive data speeds up or slows down. These packets are used to notify a client that it needs to either increase or decrease the size of the data being transmitted. You can think of this as someone pressing the button on a water fountain for you. If the button is pressed too much, you will not be able to catch all of the water in your mouth, so you must instruct the person to decrease the pressure on the button. On the flip side, if the person is not pressing the button hard enough, you won't be drinking as much water as you could be.

Next, we see our first problematic packets. As the download starts, we begin to see *TCP Previous segment lost packets*, as shown in Figure 8-4.

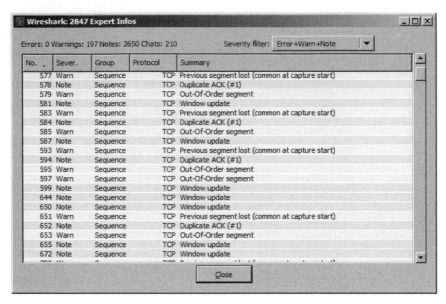

Figure 8-4: Previous segment lost packets indicate a problem.

These packets tell us that during the course of data transfer, a packet was suddenly dropped. In response, the client sends *Duplicate ACK* packets to the server, requesting that that the lost packet be sent again. The client continues to send Duplicate ACKs until it receives the requested packet. We then see the retransmission of the dropped packet as *TCP Retransmission* in the Expert Infos window, as shown in Figure 8-5.

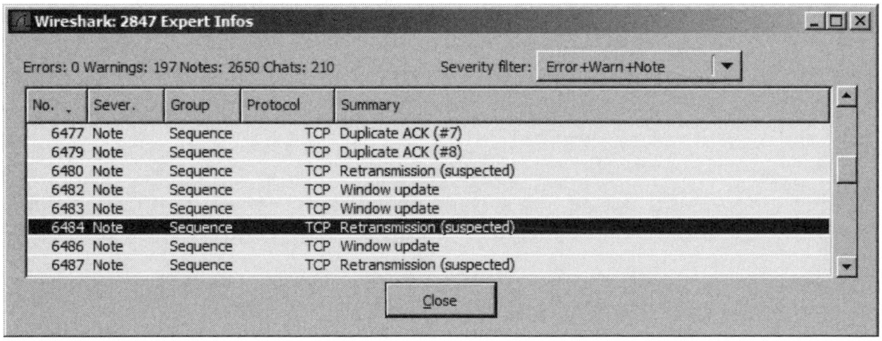

Figure 8-5: A fast retransmission is seen after a packet is dropped.

At the beginning of our download, we see only one or two Duplicate ACKs in a row, but as the download progresses, we begin to see more and more. This tells us that we are experiencing more latency. If you continue to browse through the rest of the capture, you will see that it is riddled with segment losses and Duplicate ACKs—the telltale sign of a slow download in process.

Conveniently, Wireshark allows us to graph the TCP stream for this download, as shown in Figure 8-6. You can access this graph by clicking a packet related to the stream you wish to analyze (I've selected packet number 1,023) and choosing **Statistics ▸ TCP Stream Graph ▸ Round Trip Time Graph**. The TCP Stream Graph feature of Wireshark is a great way of visualizing data throughput when dealing with a TCP stream.

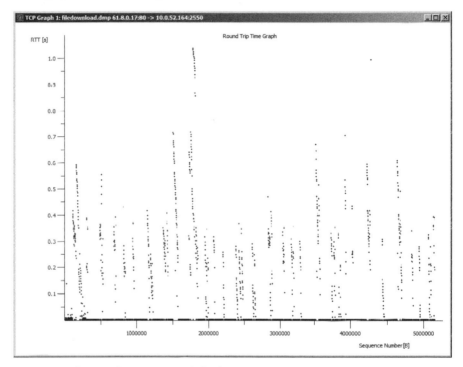

Figure 8-6: The round trip time graph for this capture

While this graph may not be aesthetically pleasing, it's a great way to compare round trip time (RTT) throughout a packet capture. Notice, for example, that near the beginning of the graph of this capture, we see RTT of more than one second. This is completely unacceptable for downloading a file. Even when downloading a file from the Internet, you should see times no greater than 0.1 seconds, with ideal times of no more than 0.04 seconds (40 milliseconds). This graph shows us right away that we've got a major problem.

A Slow Route

icmp-tracert-slow .pcap

The first step in solving any slow network problem is to determine the source of the problem. In the following scenario, the help desk has just received a call from Owen, who is complaining that his Internet connection is extremely slow.

What We Know

There isn't a whole lot that we need to know before we can begin to address this fairly straightforward complaint. We verify that the slow Internet issue persists regardless of the website visited. And, after further investigation, we learn that every machine on the same network as Owen is experiencing the problem.

Tapping into the Wire

Since Owen was the first one to complain about this issue, we will perform the analysis from his computer (though probably any computer on the network would suffice). We'll install Wireshark directly on his machine to get the packet capture we need.

Since the problem is affecting multiple computers, we know that it isn't a problem with Owen's computer specifically; a capture of just his computer trying to access the Internet won't give us the information we need. Instead, we'll use the ICMP traceroute utility to get a better idea of where the problem lies.

traceroute is an ICMP-based diagnostic tool (UDP-based under Unix) that sends packets to every router along a path, progressing until it reaches a specified destination. traceroute will report some basic information about any delays it experiences (as shown in the output in Figure 8-7), but to get a real grasp about where the bottleneck is, we will capture the results of the traceroute with Wireshark.

I have included an image of a sample traceroute output screen in Figure 8-7. Each line represents the time it takes to cross a network in route to the target destination.

```
Command Prompt                                              _ □ ×
Microsoft Windows XP [Version 5.1.2600]
(C) Copyright 1985-2001 Microsoft Corp.

c:\>tracert www.webafrica.co.za

Tracing route to www.webafrica.co.za [196.31.65.20]
over a maximum of 30 hops:

  1    <1 ms    <1 ms    <1 ms  fw1.d.barn.za.net [172.16.0.254]
  2    <1 ms    <1 ms    <1 ms  i.tsb.barn.za.net [196.7.14.112]
  3     3 ms     2 ms     2 ms  router.barn.za.net [196.7.14.110]
  4     6 ms     8 ms     8 ms  router.cabinet.barn.za.net [196.31.167.115]
  5     6 ms     8 ms     8 ms  i.cabinet.barn.za.net [196.30.11.73]
  6     7 ms     8 ms     8 ms  vlan512.hr3.cpt1.alter.net [196.31.93.49]
  7     8 ms     7 ms     8 ms  vlan10.hr1.cpt1.alter.net [196.30.176.36]
  8     8 ms     7 ms     8 ms  cpt.h-gw.net [196.7.5.134]
  9    10 ms     6 ms     7 ms  ns10.pcnets.co.za [196.31.65.20]

Trace complete.

c:\>
```

Figure 8-7: Standard traceroute output

Analysis

Looking at the capture file (icmp-tracert-slow.pcap, Figure 8-8), the first thing we see are Echo (ping) request packets being sent from Owen's computer to a remote host.

No. ▾	Time	Source	Destination	Protocol	Info
1	0.000000	24.6.126.218	198.173.244.32	ICMP	Echo (ping) request
2	3.364382	24.6.126.218	198.173.244.32	ICMP	Echo (ping) request
3	6.368126	24.6.126.218	198.173.244.32	ICMP	Echo (ping) request
4	9.371704	24.6.126.218	198.173.244.32	ICMP	Echo (ping) request

Figure 8-8: Echo (ping) request packets being sent from Owen's computer to a remote host

These packets differ from regular ping packets in one important way, as you'll see if you look under the IP section of the Packet Details pane. The difference is that the time-to-live value in these packets is set to one, as shown in Figure 8-9.

```
⊟ Internet Protocol, Src: 24.6.126.218 (24.6.126.218), Dst: 198.173.244.32 (198.173.244.32)
    Version: 4
    Header length: 20 bytes
  ⊞ Differentiated Services Field: 0x00 (DSCP 0x00: Default; ECN: 0x00)
    Total Length: 92
    Identification: 0xb5f6 (46582)
  ⊞ Flags: 0x00
    Fragment offset: 0
    Time to live: 1
    Protocol: ICMP (0x01)
  ⊞ Header checksum: 0xb1fc [correct]
    Source: 24.6.126.218 (24.6.126.218)
    Destination: 198.173.244.32 (198.173.244.32)
```

Figure 8-9: This ping packet has a time-to-live value of one.

The *time-to-live (TTL) value* is a numerical value that determines how many times a packet can hop from one router to another across a network. A value of one means that traceroute will send a packet to the destination device, but that the packet will expire once it hits the first router along the route; at that time, an ICMP TTL expired packet will be sent back. Upon receipt of this ICMP TTL expired packet, traceroute will send another packet with a TTL value of two, which will cause an ICMP TTL expired packet to be sent back once the packet hits the second router along the route. This process continues until a packet has a TTL value that is just enough to reach the destination, as illustrated in Figure 8-10.

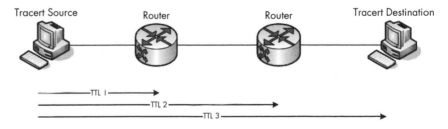

Figure 8-10: The TTL value increases as more networks are crossed en route to a destination.

Applying our newfound knowledge of TTL to our current situation, we can immediately see a problem with the first packet sent. This packet has a TTL value of one, so it should have immediately hit the internal router on our network and reported back to us—but it did not.

Since Owen's computer doesn't receive an immediate response back to the first TTL packet with value one, it waits about three seconds (as shown in Wireshark's Time field in Figure 8-11) and then sends another request.

No.	Time	Source	Destination	Protocol	Info
2	3.364382	24.6.126.218	198.173.244.32	ICMP	Echo (ping) request
3	6.368126	24.6.126.218	198.173.244.32	ICMP	Echo (ping) request

Figure 8-11: Owen's computer sends an initial request, receives no response, and sends another request three seconds later.

When Owen's computer receives no response to this second attempt, it waits about three more seconds and sends one last packet to the router, which also proves unsuccessful, as shown in Figure 8-12.

No.	Time	Source	Destination	Protocol	Info
3	6.368126	24.6.126.218	198.173.244.32	ICMP	Echo (ping) request
4	9.371704	24.6.126.218	198.173.244.32	ICMP	Echo (ping) request

Figure 8-12: After receiving no response yet again, the computer makes one more attempt.

At this point, traceroute gives up on receiving a reply from the first router, so its next packet (packet four) has a TTL value of two. This packet reaches the second router successfully, and Owen's computer receives the expected ICMP type 11, code 0 packet, which has the Time-to-live exceeded message, shown in Figure 8-13.

No.	Time	Source	Destination	Protocol	Info
5	9.393904	12.244.25.161	24.6.126.218	ICMP	Time-to-live exceeded (Time to live exceeded in transit)

Figure 8-13: This Time-to-live exceeded message is expected.

This process continues through the rest of the capture; the TTL value is continually incremented until the destination is reached.

What can we determine from this traceroute analysis? First of all, we know our problem lies with our network's internal router because we were never able to receive an ICMP response from it. Routers are very complicated devices, so we aren't going to delve into the semantics of exactly what is wrong with the router. The point is that we have successfully determined where the problem resides: in our network's internal router.

Summary

Once again, Wireshark has saved us countless hours of troubleshooting by allowing us to quickly pinpoint the source of our problem. While Wireshark won't tell us what's wrong with our router or how to fix it, we now know enough to turn our attention to the router's configuration to learn more about the problem.

We've also learned a few new things about ICMP, as well as how to work with the traceroute utility. (traceroute has several other configurable options and uses; you can find out more about them by doing a quick Internet search.)

Double Vision

double-vision
·pcap In this scenario, you have installed and configured a brand new computer for Jeff, the newest company employee. Usually, when you install a new computer, you expect it to be faster than the rest of the devices on your network. However, after only a short while, Jeff reports that during times of peak usage, his computer is experiencing severe slowness to the point that certain network services become unavailable.

What We Know

First of all, we know that Jeff's computer is brand new, so it should be running at optimal performance. Aside from that, there are no other reports of network slowness, during either peak or off-peak usage times. We also know that Jeff is a very high bandwidth user. Most of his tasks are network related, and he often runs multiple net-centric applications at once. These applications, along with standard Internet and email clients, create an above-average load of traffic, but one that our network should be able to handle easily.

Tapping into the Wire

Because this problem is related only to Jeff's computer, we will install Wireshark directly on it. The best time to analyze this problem is when it is happening, which is during peak usage time. We want Jeff to be able to perform his daily routine, so we'll start the capture file, let it run for a few minutes while Jeff does his thing, and then stop it and look at the collected data.

Analysis

The title of this scenario really becomes clear when you first open the trace file, double-vision.pcap. Immediately, you will notice two of everything—every packet in this capture file is repeated, as you can see in the beginning of the capture in Figure 8-14. This is definitely *not* normal.

NOTE *For the sake of simplicity, we'll only look at six packets, since that is really all that is required for our purposes. Just remember that all packets are duplicated for all communications from Jeff's computer.*

No.	Time	Source	Destination	Protocol	Info
1	0.000000	12.234.13.89	12.234.14.63	TCP	47063 > http [ACK] Seq=0 Ack=0 Win=4096 Len=0
2	0.025583	12.234.13.89	12.234.14.63	TCP	[TCP Dup ACK 1#1] 47063 > http [ACK] Seq=0 Ack=0 Win=4096 Len=0
3	0.025776	12.234.14.63	12.234.13.89	TCP	http > 47063 [RST] Seq=0 Len=0
4	0.066826	12.234.14.63	12.234.13.89	TCP	http > 47063 [RST] Seq=0 Len=0
5	15.001667	12.234.13.89	12.234.14.63	TCP	1093 > 424 [SYN] Seq=0 Len=0 MSS=1460
6	15.086461	12.234.13.89	12.234.14.63	TCP	1093 > 424 [SYN] Seq=0 Len=0 MSS=1460

Figure 8-14: You aren't seeing double—every packet is repeated!

There are two common causes for duplicate packets in a capture file: inconsistencies in routing and improperly configured port mirroring. Before we get down to the nitty gritty and try to determine the cause here, let's make sure the packets we are looking at are true duplicates of one another.

One way to determine whether two packets are identical is to look at the IP identification number of each in its IP header. You'll find this ID under the IP section of a packet in the Packet Details pane. You will see that the first and second packets have the same identification number, *0xc509*, as shown in Figure 8-15.

```
⊟ Internet Protocol, Src: 12.234.13.89 (12.234.13.89), Dst: 12.234.14.63 (12.234.14.63)
      Version: 4
      Header length: 20 bytes
  ⊞ Differentiated Services Field: 0x00 (DSCP 0x00: Default; ECN: 0x00)
      Total Length: 40
      Identification: 0xc509 (50441) ◄─────
  ⊞ Flags: 0x00
      Fragment offset: 0
      Time to live: 47
      Protocol: TCP (0x06)
  ⊞ Header checksum: 0x915b [correct]
      Source: 12.234.13.89 (12.234.13.89)
      Destination: 12.234.14.63 (12.234.14.63)
```

Figure 8-15: The first two packets have the same identification number.

The same is true for the third and fourth packets, which both have a transaction ID of *0xaca7*, as shown in Figure 8-16. Continuing down the list, we find that the same is true for every pair of packets in the capture file.

```
⊟ Internet Protocol, Src: 12.234.14.63 (12.234.14.63), Dst: 12.234.13.89 (12.234.13.89)
      Version: 4
      Header length: 20 bytes
  ⊞ Differentiated Services Field: 0x00 (DSCP 0x00: Default; ECN: 0x00)
      Total Length: 40
      Identification: 0xaca7 (44199) ◄─────
  ⊞ Flags: 0x00
      Fragment offset: 0
      Time to live: 128
      Protocol: TCP (0x06)
  ⊞ Header checksum: 0x58bd [correct]
      Source: 12.234.14.63 (12.234.14.63)
      Destination: 12.234.13.89 (12.234.13.89)
```

Figure 8-16: The third and fourth packets also have the same identification number.

Now that we know that all of the packets are exact duplicates as far as payload is concerned, we can begin to try to determine which of our two possible solutions is most likely to be correct—inconsistent routing or misconfigured port mirroring. To that end, we'll look at the TTL values of the packets. If these values differ, it signals an internal routing problem; if they are the same, then we probably have a port mirroring problem.

As shown in Figure 8-17, we find that the TTL value of packet 1 is 47, and the value of packet 2 is 46. This tells us that we definitely have an internal routing problem. The fact that the second packet decremented by one means that it went through a router somewhere and was then bounced back to our machine.

Because this problem is only occurring on Jeff's computer, we conclude that it must be isolated there, rather than on the network's router. After further investigation, we find that his new computer was configured with the wrong subnet mask.

```
Packet 1:
  Fragment offset: 0
  Time to live: 47
  Protocol: TCP (0x06)

Packet 2:
  Fragment offset: 0
  Time to live: 46
  Protocol: TCP (0x06)
```

Figure 8-17: The TTL values of these packets are not equal, which points to a routing problem.

Summary

If a machine is configured with the wrong subnet mask, the result can be a multitude of problems, including preventing that misconfigured computer from communicating at all. In this case, every packet sent from Jeff's computer bounced back, essentially doubling the amount of traffic the computer had to deal with and slowing communication tremendously during peak times.

Did That Server Flash Me?

http-client-refuse .pcap

Surprise! Another user is complaining about a slow Internet connection. This time, Eric complains that he cannot access a part of the Novell website to download some necessary software. Each time he visits the site, his browser loads and loads but nothing ever happens. It must be a problem with the network, right?

What We Know

After a thorough check of the network, we determine that Internet access is normal for all machines except Eric's. Therefore, the problem must be specific to Eric's workstation. His computer is running Windows, and it's completely up to date with all of the latest service packs and patches. Upon further investigation, we find that the only problem is with one particular section of the Novell website.

Tapping into the Wire

Because the problem here is only with Eric's computer, we can install Wireshark on his system and capture the packets we need. The problem occurs when he visits a particular section of the Novell website, so we'll take the trace file while this particular problem is occurring.

Analysis

When you open http-client-refuse.pcap (shown in Figure 8-18) you should be able to immediately identify it as HTTP communication, since there is an HTTP request right after the initial TCP handshake. In fact, this HTTP request looks normal until packets 28 and 29, as you'll see below. Let's step through and see if we can pinpoint the problem.

No. ▲	Time	Source	Destination	Protocol	Info
1	0.000000	67.161.32.69	130.57.5.25	TCP	1782 > http [SYN] Seq=0 Len=0 MSS=1460 WS=2
2	0.027029	130.57.5.25	67.161.32.69	TCP	http > 1782 [SYN, ACK] Seq=0 Ack=1 Win=6144 Len=0 MSS
3	0.027068	67.161.32.69	130.57.5.25	TCP	1782 > http [ACK] Seq=1 Ack=1 Win=258060 Len=0
4	0.028241	67.161.32.69	130.57.5.25	HTTP	GET /img/flash/load_stream.html?temp=1&id=webex_conve
5	0.061432	130.57.5.25	67.161.32.69	TCP	http > 1782 [ACK] Seq=1 Ack=926 Win=5219 Len=0
6	0.072229	130.57.5.25	67.161.32.69	TCP	[TCP segment of a reassembled PDU]
7	0.073391	130.57.5.25	67.161.32.69	TCP	[TCP segment of a reassembled PDU]
8	0.073430	67.161.32.69	130.57.5.25	TCP	1782 > http [ACK] Seq=926 Ack=2761 Win=258060 Len=0
9	0.074556	130.57.5.25	67.161.32.69	TCP	[TCP segment of a reassembled PDU]
10	0.074752	130.57.5.25	67.161.32.69	TCP	[TCP segment of a reassembled PDU]
11	0.074770	67.161.32.69	130.57.5.25	TCP	1782 > http [ACK] Seq=926 Ack=4301 Win=258060 Len=0

Figure 8-18: The capture begins with standard HTTP communication.

Keep an eye on the Time column in this capture. All packets are received without unusual delays until packet 28. We're in the middle of an HTTP transaction when suddenly there is a 9-second lag between packets 27 and 28.

In the world of network communications, a 9-second delay between packets is completely unacceptable, unless you are waiting for some form of user input. After 9 seconds pass, the server can no longer transmit the data it needs to send back to the client, so it sends a RST packet to terminate the connection. Our client hasn't given up yet, and he waits an additional 55 seconds (as shown in Figure 8-19) before acknowledging the reset.

No. ▲	Time	Source	Destination	Protocol	Info
28	0.000000	216.52.17.206	67.161.32.69	TCP	http > 1783 [RST] Seq=0 Len=0
29	55.834680	67.161.32.69	130.57.5.25	TCP	1782 > http [RST, ACK] Seq=0 Ack=0 Win=0 Len=0

Figure 8-19: Packets 28 and 29 present a problem.

The server has ceased to communicate with the client, and we have to find out why. We could go through the entire capture step by step and examine each packet, but that would be an extremely long and tedious process. Instead, we'll take the easy way out.

Since we are dealing with an HTTP transaction, the TCP stream should be easily readable as long as we can follow the trace file. Once you open the TCP stream, notice that different colors are used to show the communication: Red is used for data transferred from our client, and blue is used to show data transferred from the remote webserver.

Looking at this traffic, do you see anything other than normal HTML being transferred? If you browse down to the second section of traffic coming from our client, you see a request to get a Flash applet from the Novell server, as shown in Figure 8-20. This is where the problem lies. The web page Owen is trying to view is apparently making a request for a Flash object; this kind of request can be very easily blocked by a pop-up blocker. That's just what is happening here.

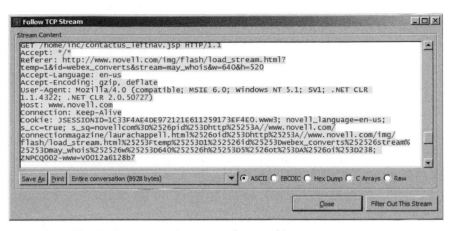

Figure 8-20: This Flash request is the source of our problem.

Summary

After a bit of research into the Flash data being called from the Novell site, you learn that the site attempts to open its main content in a new Flash window, which Eric's pop-up blocker in Internet Explorer is blocking. While the browser was unable to give us any useful information about the problem (other than a connection timeout message), we used Wireshark, some basic packet analysis concepts, and a little patience to pinpoint the exact spot where the communication process was being hindered.

A Torrential Downfall

**torrential-
slowness.pcap**

In this next scenario, one of our network users has just called the help desk complaining that the network is running extremely slowly. He can't access the Internet or any net-centric applications at a reasonable speed, and he's getting really behind in his work. What's slowing things down?

What We Know

After surveying other network users we learn that the Internet problem is widespread. All users report that the Internet is so slow that it is almost unusable. The edge router of your network also indicates high processor utilization, showing that it is handling very substantial traffic, both outbound and inbound.

NOTE   *The phrase* edge router *describes the location of a router on a network. An edge router sits on the network and connects that network to the outside world.*

Tapping into the Wire

Because the edge router handles all traffic between the local network and the Internet, and because it shows high processor load, the edge router is the best point of analysis here.

Analysis

We'll use port mirroring to tackle this scenario, because we obviously can't install Wireshark on a router.

The packets included in the capture torrential-slowness.pcap offer only a brief sampling of the many connections happening on our network, as shown in Figure 8-21.

No.	Time	Source	Destination	Protocol	Info
1	0.000000	203.211.67.195	192.168.0.193	TCP	11766 > 1534 [PSH, ACK] Seq=0 Ack=0 Win=65535 Len=1418
2	0.000033	192.168.0.193	203.211.67.195	TCP	1534 > 11766 [ACK] Seq=7090 Ack=4294965878 Win=65535 Len=0
3	0.000053	124.197.17.30	192.168.0.193	TCP	26507 > 4512 [ACK] Seq=0 Ack=0 Win=64227 Len=0
4	0.000070	192.168.0.193	124.197.17.30	TCP	4512 > 26507 [PSH, ACK] Seq=8117 Ack=0 Win=65108 Len=1380
5	0.000121	213.17.90.77	192.168.0.193	TCP	14173 > 3331 [ACK] Seq=0 Ack=0 Win=65535 Len=0
6	0.000136	192.168.0.193	213.17.90.77	TCP	3331 > 14173 [PSH, ACK] Seq=216 Ack=0 Win=65492 Len=1452
7	0.000147	192.168.0.193	213.17.90.77	TCP	3331 > 14173 [PSH, ACK] Seq=1668 Ack=0 Win=65492 Len=1452
8	0.009806	189.142.91.6	192.168.0.193	TCP	3326 > 6881 [ACK] Seq=0 Ack=0 Win=64240 Len=0
9	0.009844	192.168.0.193	189.142.91.6	TCP	6881 > 3326 [PSH, ACK] Seq=8280 Ack=0 Win=65006 Len=1380
10	0.025255	142.68.42.31	192.168.0.193	TCP	6881 > 4853 [ACK] Seq=0 Ack=0 Win=17280 Len=0

Figure 8-21: There are a lot of connection attempts in this capture.

One system inside our network (192.168.0.193) appears repeatedly in this capture, making and receiving connections from a lot of systems outside our network. More ominously, most of that traffic is being sent with the TCP PSH flag on, which forces a receiving computer to skip its buffer and push that traffic straight through, ahead of any other traffic. This is almost always a bad sign.

Still worse, most of these connections are already past the TCP handshake phase, meaning they are actively transferring data to and from our client. You can get a sense of how many of these connections are taking place by looking at the Conversations dialog shown in Figure 8-22.

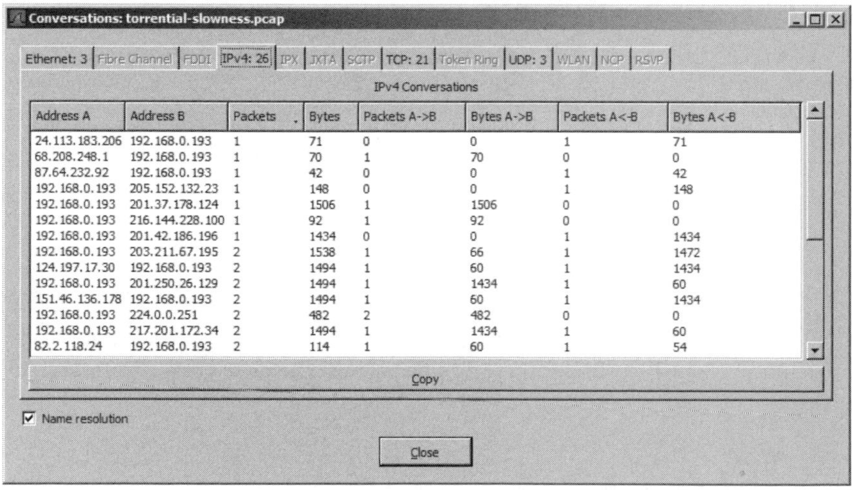

Address A	Address B	Packets	Bytes	Packets A->B	Bytes A->B	Packets A<-B	Bytes A<-B
24.113.183.206	192.168.0.193	1	71	0	0	1	71
68.208.248.1	192.168.0.193	1	70	1	70	0	0
87.64.232.92	192.168.0.193	1	42	0	0	1	42
192.168.0.193	205.152.132.23	1	148	0	0	1	148
192.168.0.193	201.37.178.124	1	1506	1	1506	0	0
192.168.0.193	216.144.228.100	1	92	1	92	0	0
192.168.0.193	201.42.186.196	1	1434	0	0	1	1434
192.168.0.193	203.211.67.195	2	1538	1	66	1	1472
124.197.17.30	192.168.0.193	2	1494	1	60	1	1434
192.168.0.193	201.250.26.129	2	1494	1	1434	1	60
151.46.136.178	192.168.0.193	2	1494	1	60	1	1434
192.168.0.193	224.0.0.251	2	482	2	482	0	0
192.168.0.193	217.201.172.34	2	1494	1	1434	1	60
82.2.118.24	192.168.0.193	2	114	1	60	1	54

Figure 8-22: The Conversations dialog shows that a lot of conversations are happening.

In just this small, 1-second capture, there are 27 different TCP conversations taking place!

The simplest way to alleviate this problem would be to go to the offending computer and poke around, but what fun would that be? We'll do things the packet analysis way.

Looking at the packets, your first course of action might be to track down the remote IP addresses and see where they are located, typically by performing a WHOIS lookup on each IP address. However, in this case you would quickly find that most of these IP addresses do not point to any companies or even to the same general area, but rather to different locations around the world.

To further evaluate the packets, you could see whether the TCP stream holds any valuable information. In this case, following the TCP stream proves useless—the data shown is gibberish, as you can see in Figure 8-23.

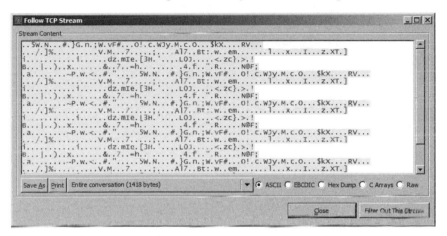

Figure 8-23: The TCP stream doesn't provide anything of real value.

When these highly technical means of tracking things down fail, what are you to do? How about the simplest thing possible (other than poking around on the suspect machine)? Simply scroll down the list of packets, one by one, and look for something significant.

As you scroll through the packets in the capture, you will eventually find yourself at packet 99, shown in Figure 8-24. This packet identifies the culprit by querying remote BitTorrent servers, as shown in the Info field. This popular peer-to-peer file transfer service is the source of our problem and all of these connections.

No. ▾	Time	Source	Destination	Protocol	Info
99	0.774636	192.168.0.193	224.0.0.251	MDNS	Standard query PTR _BitTorrent-e7393164158de2fac0f58a13a0f

Figure 8-24: Stepping through individual packets leads us to the culprit, BitTorrent.

Summary

In this case, a user installed BitTorrent on his workstation to download music and configured it to allow both incoming and outgoing connections at an unlimited rate. This high amount of bandwidth allowed one workstation to monopolize all of the company's Internet traffic.

This case reminds us that when doing analysis, it is common to want to use some of the more advanced features to try to quickly solve the problem; however, sometimes the quickest solution is to simply examine individual packets.

POP Goes the Email Server

email-troubles
.pcap

In terms of importance, email ranks right up there with the Internet in the eyes of employees. That being the case, when it's not working, you are going to hear about it.

In this scenario, all of the users on your network are complaining that their email is taking an extremely long time to reach its destination. While this is sometimes the case with email sent to other domains, even email they send to fellow employees within the same organization is taking forever. Let's get to the bottom of this.

What We Know

All email in our company is managed through one mail server. After doing some research, we confirm that this problem exists for all of the email clients in our network. Whereas a typical intra-office email would normally be delivered instantaneously, delivery is now taking from 10 to 15 minutes. The same delay is true for the receipt of external email.

Tapping into the Wire

Because our problem relates to a service that is hosted on one machine, the mail server, we'll place our analyzer there. The problem has so far been consistent throughout the work day, so any time is a good time to capture packets.

Analysis

When you look at the results of the capture (email-troubles.pcap) you will see exactly what you should see on an email server: email packets. There are a whole lot of Post Office Protocol (POP) packets coming into our mail server (see Figure 8-25), but just how many and at what rate? Perhaps our mail server is being overloaded.

No. ▾	Time	Source	Destination	Protocol	Info
1	0.000000	12.234.13.202	161.58.73.170	POP	Request: RETR 20
2	0.079320	161.58.73.170	12.234.13.202	TCP	pop3 > 1567 [ACK] Seq=0 Ack=9 Win=49152 Len=0
3	0.090650	161.58.73.170	12.234.13.202	POP	Response: +OK 100220 octets
4	0.091089	161.58.73.170	12.234.13.202	POP	Continuation
5	0.091117	12.234.13.202	161.58.73.170	TCP	1567 > pop3 [ACK] Seq=9 Ack=2920 Win=64512 Len=0
6	0.092467	161.58.73.170	12.234.13.202	POP	Continuation

Figure 8-25: This capture includes a lot of POP packets.

To determine the rate at which we're receiving POP packets, change the time display format to **Seconds Since Beginning of Capture** and look at the last packet in the file. This result tells us that we are looking at about two minutes' worth of traffic, as shown in the Time column in Figure 8-26.

No. ▾	Time	Source	Destination	Protocol	Info
360	121.664143	12.234.13.202	161.58.73.170	TCP	1567 > pop3 [ACK] Seq=27 Ack=301035 Win=63337 Len=0

Figure 8-26: Changing the time display format gives us an idea of how much data we are receiving in what amount of time.

Now we can start to look at each communication stream to see if anything abnormal is going on.

The great thing about a POP packet is that if you want to view the contents of the email message it contains, all you have to do is view the TCP stream associated with it. For example, if you do this for packet 1, you'll see that this email includes text as well as an attachment, document_9446.pif, as shown in Figure 8-27.

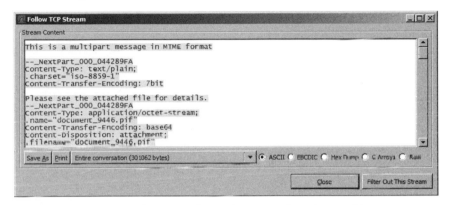

Figure 8-27: The details of packet 1 show information about the email being sent.

Looking further through this stream, we see another message from another suspicious-looking email address; it also has a PIF file attached to it.

A quick search for *PIF files* will tell you that these are Program Information Files—not something you should typically see coming through email. Not only that, but these files tend to be very large executables. Over the course of this capture file, these files just keep coming in, from multiple sources.

What we have here is an influx of spam (and possibly virus- or worm-containing) email that is overloading our email server and slowing email traffic across the network.

Summary

Our email server is being overwhelmed by a high volume of spam with large attachments. This condition is very commonly seen when monitoring email server performance. As an organization grows, the amount of spam received grows with it. In the case of our network, the users can either be patient and ride out the slowness, or the organization can invest in some sort of enterprise spam-filtering solution.

Here's Something Gnu

gnutella.pcap This scenario is along the same lines as our earlier BitTorrent scenario. Tina, a user on our network, calls and complains that her computer is running incredibly slowly, whether she's doing something locally, over the local network, or over the Internet.

What We Know

This scenario presents the same case as our earlier BitTorrent example. As such, we know that this problem is widespread and is affecting other users, as well. However, the other users are only reporting slow speeds when dealing with the Internet and net-centric applications. The edge router on our network is reporting high processor utilization and a large amount of inbound and outbound traffic.

Tapping into the Wire

In this case, all of the symptoms of the affected computers are consistent with our BitTorrent example, with the exception of Tina's computer. Not only are her net-centric applications slow, but her computer is dragging a bit in general.

Because her computer is showing unique symptoms, we assume that the problem is related to her computer, so that's where we'll begin our analysis. However, with Tina's computer running so slowly, installing Wireshark directly on it might not be the best idea—her computer's sluggishness could cause packets to be lost in the capture process. We'll use port mirroring instead.

Analysis

This capture file (gnutella.pcap) is long, but looks a lot like the BitTorrent capture, for the most part. As you can see in Figure 8-28, Tina's computer, 10.1.4.176, appears to be trying to communicate with several different hosts outside of our network. Most of these attempts either come back unanswered after the initial SYN or are denied by the client with a RST packet.

No. ⋅	Time	Source	Destination	Protocol	Info
1	0.000000	10.1.4.176	66.68.99.53	TCP	3663 > 6346 [SYN] Seq=0 Len=0 MSS=1460
2	0.028257	10.1.4.176	198.82.59.65	TCP	3684 > 6346 [SYN] Seq=0 Len=0 MSS=1460
3	0.060831	198.82.59.65	10.1.4.176	TCP	6346 > 3684 [RST, ACK] Seq=0 Ack=1 Win=0 Len=0
4	0.499894	10.1.4.176	198.82.59.65	TCP	3684 > 6346 [SYN] Seq=0 Len=0 MSS=1460
5	0.531212	198.82.59.65	10.1.4.176	TCP	6346 > 3684 [RST, ACK] Seq=0 Ack=1 Win=0 Len=0
6	0.999962	10.1.4.176	198.82.59.65	TCP	3684 > 6346 [SYN] Seq=0 Len=0 MSS=1460
7	1.030592	198.82.59.65	10.1.4.176	TCP	6346 > 3684 [RST, ACK] Seq=0 Ack=1 Win=0 Len=0

Figure 8-28: Most of these TCP connection attempts are failures.

Several things could be causing these connections to fail, but before we investigate further, lets see exactly how much traffic we are contending with so that we can determine the extent of our problem. A good way to do at this is to look at the Conversations dialog to see how many individual TCP and IP conversations are going on, as shown in Figure 8-29.

The Conversations window shows that this trace file contains 81 IP conversations and 243 TCP conversations, as you can see in the tabs at the top of Figure 8-29. This large number of conversations is usually acceptable if you are viewing traffic captured from a server, but this is a workstation; it's not normal to see this many conversations over such a short a period of time.

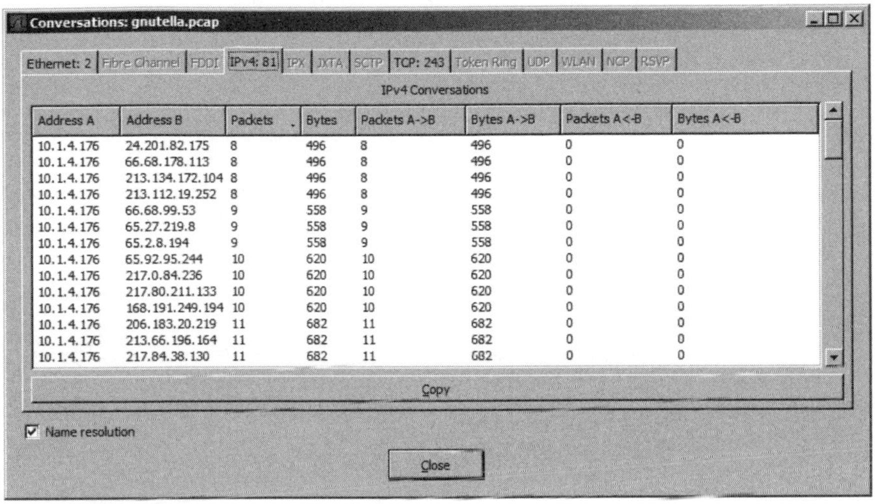

Figure 8-29: The Conversations dialog shows that a lot of conversations are happening.

If you look at some of these TCP conversations, you will see that every one involves a remote host. You can tell that most of these conversations were not successful, since the number of packets for each is very low.

In order to get the information we really need to evaluate the communication going on here, we need to see a successful conversation. The best way to do so is from the Conversations window that we already have open. With the **IPv4: 81** tab selected in that window, click the **Packets** heading to sort all conversations by the number of packets they contain, as shown in Figure 8-30.

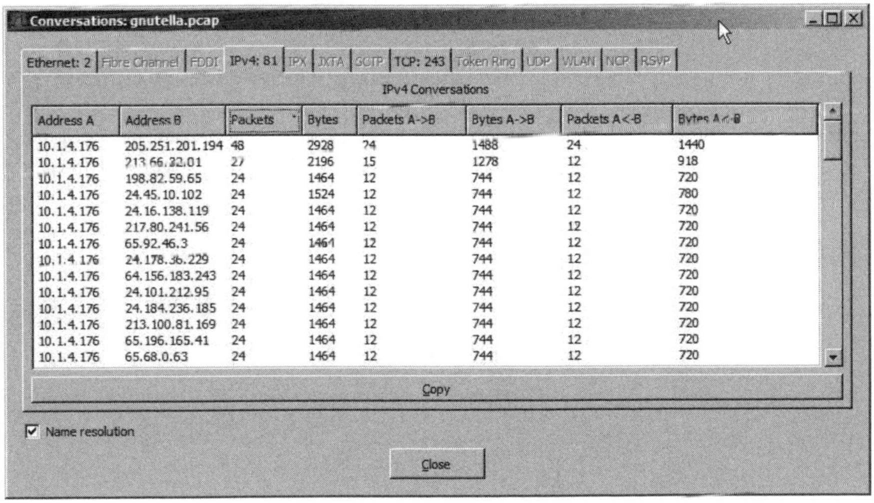

Figure 8-30: A view showing the conversations sorted by the number of packets they contain

You should see communication between Tina's computer and the remote host, 65.34.1.56, at the top of the list, as shown in Figure 8-31.

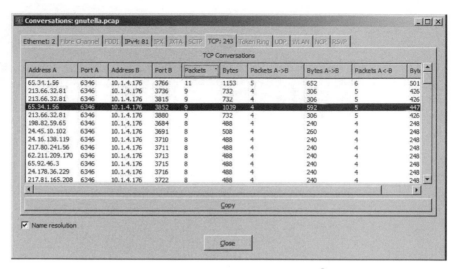

Figure 8-31: Tina's computer and a remote host communicate here.

Now, view only these packets by right-clicking this conversation, selecting **Apply as Selected**, selecting **Apply a Filter**, and then choosing **A<->B**. The result is that you see only the packets shown in Figure 8-32.

No.	Time	Source	Destination	Protocol	Info
426	52.436286	10.1.4.176	65.34.1.56	TCP	3766 > 6346 [SYN] Seq=0 Len=0 MSS=1460
429	52.514080	65.34.1.56	10.1.4.176	TCP	6346 > 3766 [SYN, ACK] Seq=0 Ack=1 Win=17520 Len=0 MSS=1460
430	52.514799	10.1.4.176	65.34.1.56	TCP	3766 > 6346 [ACK] Seq=1 Ack=1 Win=8760 Len=0
431	52.515422	10.1.4.176	65.34.1.56	Gnutel	
432	52.722234	65.34.1.56	10.1.4.176	TCP	6346 > 3766 [ACK] Seq=1 Ack=31 Win=17490 Len=0
433	52.724068	10.1.4.176	65.34.1.56	Gnutel	
434	52.844222	65.34.1.56	10.1.4.176	Gnutel	

Figure 8-32: Now only the packets in the relevant conversation are shown.

The packets shown in Figure 8-32 offer some additional information that leads us straight to the problem. Specifically, packets 431, 433, and 434 are all identified as Gnutel packets. These Gnutel packets are characteristic of traffic sent or received through the Gnutella file-sharing network. Clicking them gives a bit more detail, as shown in Figure 8-33.

```
⊞ Transmission Control Protocol, Src Port: 3766 (3766), Dst Port: 6346 (6346), Seq: 1, Ack: 1, Len: 30
⊟ Gnutella Protocol
    Gnutella Upload / Download Stream
```

Figure 8-33: These Gnutella packets contain some interesting information.

The Packet Details pane for packet 431 (in Figure 8-33) doesn't really give us any useful information, other than that this packet is a Download/Upload stream traversing the Gnutella network. If we look at the Packet Bytes pane (Figure 8-34), however, we see something a bit alarming.

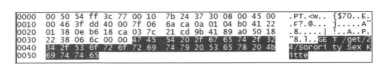

```
0000  00 50 54 ff 3c 77 00 10  7b 24 37 30 08 00 45 00   .PT.<w.. {$70..E.
0010  00 46 3f dd 40 00 7f 06  6a ca 0a 01 04 b0 41 22   .F?.@... j.....A"
0020  01 38 0e b6 18 ca 03 7c  21 cd 9b 41 89 a0 50 18   .8.....| !..A..P.
0030  22 38 06 6c 00 00 47 45  54 20 2f 67 65 74 2f 32   "8.l..GE T /get/2
0040  34 2f 53 6f 72 6f 72 69  74 79 20 53 65 78 20 4b   4/Sorori ty Sex K
0050  69 74 74 65                                        itte
```

Figure 8-34: The Packet Bytes pane shows us what is being downloaded through Gnutella.

This particular data stream shows a GET command downloading a file with a name containing the words *sorority sex kitten*. We have found our suspect traffic.

As a brief aside, here's another way to tell that this is Gnutella traffic. If you look at all of the conversation attempts taking place, you will notice that the Info heading of the Packet List pane shows all of this communication happening on port 6346, as shown in Figure 8-35.

No. ▲	Time	Source	Destination	Protocol	Info
583	75.544302	10.1.4.176	65.27.229.23	TCP	3803 > 6346 [SYN] Seq=0 Len=0 MSS=1460
584	75.544499	10.1.4.176	74.28.233.147	TCP	3802 > 6346 [SYN] Seq=0 Len=0 MSS=1460
585	75.544750	10.1.4.176	65.2.243.188	TCP	3801 > 6346 [SYN] Seq=0 Len=0 MSS=1460
586	75.545190	10.1.4.176	24.178.197.5	TCP	3804 > 6346 [SYN] Seq=0 Len=0 MSS=1460
587	75.545446	10.1.4.176	24.249.29.119	TCP	3799 > 6346 [SYN] Seq=0 Len=0 MSS=1460

Figure 8-35: Looking at the port number is a good way to identify the type of traffic.

A quick search for this port number at http://www.iana.org will list the services associated with this port.

Summary

The Gnutella network is commonly used for the downloading and distribution of various file types. This idea may sound great at first, but unfortunately, it has resulted in a large peer-to-peer network of pornography as well as pirated software, movies, and music.

In this scenario, it seems that Tina, or someone using Tina's computer, has installed some form of Gnutella client in order to download pornographic material.

Final Thoughts

If you look at way each of these scenarios was resolved, you will notice that most of the problems were not actually network related. This is pretty common when it comes to complaints about a slow network. Typically, it isn't the network that is slow, but rather problems with individual computers or applications that make users perceive it that way.

9

SECURITY-BASED ANALYSIS

In this chapter we'll dive into several
security-related network scenarios and work
through them with Wireshark. With looming
threats of hackers, identity thieves, and corporate
data theft, you can't afford *not* to be able to analyze the
security of your network at the packet level.

OS Fingerprinting

osfingerprinting
.pcap
Operating system (OS) fingerprinting is a technique used by hackers to identify
a remote computer's operating system in order to gain information that
could be useful for breaking into it. OS fingerprinting works by using a
remote machine to send various commands to a target computer. When
the remote machine receives the responses to these commands, it can interpret those responses to make an educated guess at the operating system the
target computer is using. Knowing the operating system of a computer you
wish to exploit allows you to quickly find exploits specific to that operating
system.

When you open osfingerprinting.pcap, you'll see several different types of ICMP traffic, as shown in Figure 9-1. Some of this traffic, like Echo (ping) request and Echo (ping) reply, are common and should not be cause for alarm. However, traffic like *Timestamp request/reply*, *Address mask request*, and *Information request* is unusual.

No. ▴	Time	Source	Destination	Protocol	Info
11	1.863030	10.0.0.29	10.0.0.2	ICMP	Timestamp request
12	1.863238	10.0.0.2	10.0.0.29	ICMP	Timestamp reply
13	1.869470	10.0.0.29	10.0.0.2	ICMP	Timestamp request
14	1.869609	10.0.0.2	10.0.0.29	ICMP	Timestamp reply
15	2.739445	10.0.0.29	10.0.0.2	ICMP	Address mask request
16	2.742531	10.0.0.29	10.0.0.2	ICMP	Address mask request
17	7.062589	10.0.0.29	10.0.0.2	ICMP	Information request
18	7.064628	10.0.0.29	10.0.0.2	ICMP	Information request
19	11.354823	10.0.0.29	10.0.0.2	ICMP	Echo (ping) request
20	11.355045	10.0.0.2	10.0.0.29	ICMP	Echo (ping) reply
21	11.359669	10.0.0.29	10.0.0.2	ICMP	Echo (ping) request
22	11.359816	10.0.0.2	10.0.0.29	ICMP	Echo (ping) reply

Figure 9-1: This is the kind of ICMP traffic you don't want to see.

The unusual ICMP request traffic that we see in Figure 9-1 suggests that our system is the target of an attacker using ICMP-based OS fingerprinting scans. An attacker sends these requests and uses the target system's response (if there is any) to determine the specific operating system running on the target.

NOTE *Because we should never see ICMP types 13, 15, or 17 traffic under normal circumstances, we can create a filter that will show only those types of traffic so we can check for it quickly. This filter is* icmp .type==13 || icmp .type==15 || icmp .type==17.

A Simple Port Scan

portscan.pcap   Attackers can use port scans to learn very critical information about a network. Using specialized port-scanning software, a hacker can attempt to connect to a device on a specified array of ports, such as 21 (FTP) and 80 (HTTP). With the information received from these scans, an attacker can find open ports that could allow access to your network. Think of an open port as a secret tunnel into a well-guarded castle. Once a hacker knows about one of these tunnels, he may very well be able to get in using the right bag of tricks. Figure 9-2, based on the capture portscan.pcap, shows a port scan at work.

No. ▴	Time	Source	Destination	Protocol	Info
7	0.607512	10.100.25.14	10.100.18.12	TCP	16748 > telnet [SYN] Seq=0 Len=0
8	0.707986	10.100.25.14	10.100.18.12	TCP	12502 > ftp [SYN] Seq=0 Len=0
9	0.808340	10.100.25.14	10.100.18.12	TCP	30382 > 6000 [SYN] Seq=0 Len=0
10	0.904949	10.100.25.14	10.100.18.12	TCP	27986 > 1025 [SYN] Seq=0 Len=0
11	1.004235	10.100.25.14	10.100.18.12	TCP	25488 > smtp [SYN] Seq=0 Len=0
12	1.110883	10.100.25.14	10.100.18.12	TCP	6729 > sunrpc [SYN] Seq=0 Len=0
13	1.212836	10.100.25.14	10.100.18.12	TCP	29169 > 1028 [SYN] Seq=0 Len=0
14	1.307771	10.100.25.14	10.100.18.12	TCP	24305 > 9100 [SYN] Seq=0 Len=0
15	1.407052	10.100.25.14	10.100.18.12	TCP	17851 > 1029 [SYN] Seq=0 Len=0
16	1.512738	10.100.25.14	10.100.18.12	TCP	10985 > finger [SYN] Seq=0 Len=0

Figure 9-2: A port scan shows multiple connection attempts on various ports.

As you can see in Figure 9-2, there are quite a few packets traveling between 10.100.25.14 (the local machine) and 10.100.18.12 (a remote computer). When you take a closer look at these packets, you will see exactly why they are so suspicious.

Our trace file shows that every packet sent from the remote computer is being sent to a different port number on the local machine (for example, 21 and 1028).

But more importantly, these ports happen to be commonly exploited ones, such as telnet, microsoft-ds, FTP, and SMTP. When you see a remote computer sending multiple packets to commonly exploited ports, you can typically assume that a port scan is taking place.

The Flooded Printer

printerproblem
.pcap

Even the smallest organizations can have several networked printers. Factor in the cost of paper, ink, and maintenance, and the total cost of ownership for even a low-volume network printer can add up quickly.

In this scenario one of the higher-volume network printers on our network has begun printing out complete garbage, and nobody knows the source of it. Our goal is to find the source of these mystery documents and put an end to it.

What We Know

Our printer is a high-volume network printer shared through a server. It has no special permissions assigned to it nor any extra logging capabilities. The problem is constant. Even when we clear out the printer's queue, it fills up immediately and starts printing again.

Tapping into the Wire

Because the problem printer is installed on a server, there will be a lot of traffic flowing around the wire, and we'll have a lot of data to sort through. Regardless, installing Wireshark directly on the server is the best way to go. Since the problem seems to be constant, we can capture packets at any time.

Analysis

The capture file printerproblem.pcap is a pretty good example of what traffic to a printer looks like. As you can see in Figure 9-3, our server, 10.100.16.15, is receiving a massive influx of SPOOLS packets from a client within our network, 10.100.17.47.

No. -	Time	Source	Destination	Protocol	Info
49	0.058610	10.100.17.47	10.100.16.15	SPOOLS	DeletePrinterIC request
50	0.058679	10.100.16.15	10.100.17.47	SPOOLS	DeletePrinterIC response
51	0.059582	10.100.17.47	10.100.16.15	SPOOLS	OpenPrinterEx request, \\e205000n5\Tech-office
52	0.059799	10.100.16.15	10.100.17.47	SPOOLS	OpenPrinterEx response
53	0.060312	10.100.17.47	10.100.16.15	SPOOLS	ClosePrinter request
54	0.060396	10.100.16.15	10.100.17.47	SPOOLS	ClosePrinter response
55	0.061042	10.100.17.47	10.100.16.15	SPOOLS	StartDocPrinter request, OpenPrinterEx(\\e205000n5\Tech-office)
56	0.062040	10.100.16.15	10.100.17.47	SPOOLS	StartDocPrinter response

Figure 9-3: All of the SPOOLS traffic is going to the printer.

It's easy enough to identify the source of the printing in this case, but we still haven't solved the problem. To learn more about what's happening, let's view the TCP stream of data being sent to the printer. When you do, you'll see that the data is being printed from Microsoft Word and that the username of the person printing the data is *csanders* (Figure 9-4).

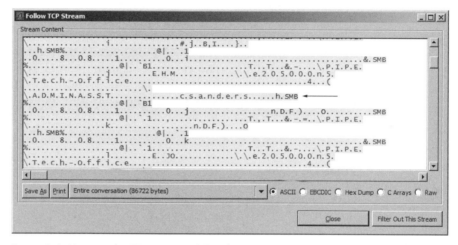

Figure 9-4: Viewing the TCP stream of data being sent to a printer can give good insight.

Summary

While we haven't stopped the influx of SPOOLS packets in this scenario, we have used Wireshark to quickly find the source of our mysterious printer problem. Having identified the source, we can find out why this information is being sent to the printer. (Most likely, client 10.100.17.47 on our network has been compromised in some way.)

An FTP Break-In

ftp-crack.pcap   FTP is one of the most commonly used means of transferring large amounts of data. The company we will be looking at now has an internal FTP server that it uses to maintain all of its pre-release software. Lately, the IT technician in charge of maintaining and monitoring this server has noticed a large amount of traffic on the server after hours. Unfortunately, the FTP server software doesn't have logging functionality, so the only way to get a good grasp of what is going on is to get a packet capture. We want to identify the reason for the server's increase in bandwidth and eliminate the source.

What We Know

The FTP server is running very old software with no decent logging functionality. All major developers within the company have usernames and accounts that allow them full access to all files on the server. This server is also configured so that it may be accessed from outside of the network so that developers can work from home.

Tapping into the Wire

Since this server is on our network, installing Wireshark on it may seem like the best method to use. However, since the server is experiencing a very high traffic load, packets might be dropped if we bog down the server too much, so we'll use port mirroring instead.

Analysis

When you open the capture ftp-crack.pcap, you will see a whole lot happening in a very short amount of time. From our discussion of FTP in Chapter 6, you should be familiar with how the FTP authentication process should look.

After the initial TCP handshake, a login process will typically take place so that the user can begin interacting with the server. In this capture, we jump right into a username and password authentication process, and as you can see in packet 4 (Figure 9-5), this authentication attempt fails.

```
⊟ File Transfer Protocol (FTP)
  ⊟ 530 Login incorrect.\r\n
      Response code: Not logged in (530)
      Response arg: Login incorrect.
```

Figure 9-5: Packet 4 shows the first authentication attempt failure.

We might assume that the user trying to log in has mistyped his password, but that assumption is quickly put to rest in the next several packets. As shown in Figure 9-6, we see lots of authentication failures.

No. ·	Time	Source	Destination	Protocol	Info
27	0.104111	10.121.70.151	10.234.125.254	TCP	ftp > 2220 [FIN, ACK] Seq=22 Ack=1 Win=49152 [TCP CHECKSUM INCORRECT] Len=0
28	0.104155	10.121.70.151	10.234.125.254	TCP	2220 > ftp [ACK] Seq=1 Ack=23 Win=17447 [TCP CHECKSUM INCORRECT] Len=0
29	0.108560	10.121.70.151	10.234.125.254	FTP	Response: 530 Login incorrect. ◄———
30	0.108773	10.121.70.151	10.234.125.254	TCP	ftp > 2221 [ACK] Seq=34 Ack=14 Win=49152 [TCP CHECKSUM INCORRECT] Len=0
31	0.112332	10.234.125.254	10.121.70.151	TCP	2222 > ftp [FIN, ACK] Seq=13 Ack=56 Win=17447 [TCP CHECKSUM INCORRECT] Len=0
32	0.120024	10.121.70.151	10.234.125.254	FTP	Response: 530 Login incorrect. ◄———
33	0.121851	10.234.125.254	10.121.70.151	TCP	2221 > ftp [FIN, ACK] Seq=14 Ack=56 Win=17447 [TCP CHECKSUM INCORRECT] Len=0
34	0.122830	10.121.70.151	10.234.125.254	TCP	ftp > 2223 [ACK] Seq=34 Ack=11 Win=49152 [TCP CHECKSUM INCORRECT] Len=0
35	0.141432	10.121.70.151	10.234.125.254	TCP	ftp > 2222 [ACK] Seq=56 Ack=14 Win=49152 [TCP CHECKSUM INCORRECT] Len=0
36	0.141886	10.121.70.151	10.234.125.254	TCP	ftp > 2222 [FIN, ACK] Seq=56 Ack=14 Win=49152 [TCP CHECKSUM INCORRECT] Len=0
37	0.141939	10.234.125.254	10.121.70.151	TCP	2222 > ftp [ACK] Seq=14 Ack=57 Win=17447 [TCP CHECKSUM INCORRECT] Len=0
38	0.145312	10.234.125.254	10.121.70.151	TCP	ftp > 2221 [ACK] Seq=56 Ack=15 Win=49152 [TCP CHECKSUM INCORRECT] Len=0
39	0.145896	10.121.70.151	10.234.125.254	FTP	Response: 530 Login incorrect. ◄———

Figure 9-6: You immediately begin seeing a lot of authentication failures.

Immediately following the failed authentication attempt, we see another login attempt to the server (10.121.70.151) from a client within our own network (10.234.125.254). The odd thing about this request is that the user is attempting to log in using the admin account, as seen in packet 10 in Figure 9-7.

```
⊟ File Transfer Protocol (FTP)
  ⊟ 331 Password required for admin.\r\n
      Response code: User name okay, need password (331)
      Response arg: Password required for admin.
```

Figure 9-7: Packet 10 shows an attempt to log in to the admin account.

This is a great opportunity to use a display filter to show only those packets that represent an FTP login attempt, like so:

```
ftp.request.command == "USER" || ftp.request.command == "PASS"
```

Figure 9-8 shows the result of using this filter.

Figure 9-8: The short display filter entered into the Display Filter window helps to show only relevant traffic.

Now, if we look in the Info column of each login attempt, we can see that the passwords being used are in alphabetical order—that is, the attacker is stepping through each letter of the alphabet in succession. This is a tell-tale sign that someone is trying to guess the password of an account using a dictionary-style attack. A *dictionary attack* is one in which passwords are guessed based upon a user- or machine-created dictionary of words. If you look at the time between each attempt, you can also see that these attempts to guess the password are happening too quickly to be entered by a human; they're most likely being launched by a cracking tool. We have successfully found the source of our high-bandwidth utilization.

Summary

We have confirmed that a machine within our network is being attacked by a cracking program designed to perform a dictionary attack on the FTP server. But our job isn't done yet. At this point you must determine whether the employee whose machine is launching the attack is responsible for orchestrating it or if the machine has been compromised from the outside.

Blaster Worm

blaster.pcap The looming threat of viruses and worms spreading across the Internet is one that frightens system administrators and end users alike. In this scenario, Eddy calls the help desk with concerns that his computer has been infected with a virus. Every time he starts his computer, he receives a message that it will shut down in 60 seconds. Once this 60-second timer expires, the computer shuts down as stated. This process keeps repeating continuously and he is not able to access his computer for more than 60 seconds at a time.

What We Know

We know that Eddy tends to be careful about security, so spyware isn't an immediate concern. Our company uses virus-scanning software; however it is decentralized and mostly user managed.

Tapping into the Wire

Any time you suspect that a virus or worm may be the cause of a computer problem, it is not usually a wise idea to install a sniffer directly on that machine. Malicious programs can often work against packet sniffers by not allowing them to run properly or at all. Our best approach here is to use port mirroring. The capture will begin as soon as the computer boots up and will finish when the computer shuts itself down after the 60-second timer expires.

Analysis

The capture file blaster.pcap, shown in Figure 9-9, records a few TCP packets being transmitted from our suspect computer to another computer on the local network via ports 1793 and 4444. These packets are captured at a time when nothing is active on the machine other than the 60-second timer, so this network activity is suspicious.

No.	Time	Source	Destination	Protocol	Info
1	0.000000	10.234.0.239	10.234.2.116	TCP	1793 > 4444 [ACK] Seq=0 Ack=0 Win=17330 [TCP C
2	0.000191	10.234.2.116	10.234.0.239	TCP	4444 > 1793 [PSH, ACK] Seq=0 Ack=0 Win=64475
3	0.218319	10.234.0.239	10.234.2.116	TCP	1793 > 4444 [ACK] Seq=0 Ack=20 Win=17310 [TCP
4	1.673435	10.234.0.239	10.234.2.116	TCP	1793 > 4444 [PSH, ACK] Seq=0 Ack=20 Win=17310
5	1.673773	10.234.2.116	10.234.0.239	TCP	4444 > 1793 [PSH, ACK] Seq=20 Ack=18 Win=64457
6	1.859752	10.234.0.239	10.234.2.116	TCP	1793 > 4444 [ACK] Seq=18 Ack=38 Win=17292 [TCP
7	3.713980	10.234.0.239	10.234.2.116	TCP	1793 > 4444 [PSH, ACK] Seq=18 Ack=38 Win=17292
8	3.900264	10.234.2.116	10.234.0.239	TCP	4444 > 1793 [ACK] Seq=38 Ack=30 Win=64445 [TCP

Figure 9-9: We shouldn't see this level of network activity with only the timer running on this machine.

One of the best ways to identify virus or worm traffic is to look at the raw data being sent across the wire. Let's look for each packet in our capture in the Packet Bytes pane at the bottom of the Wireshark main window. The raw data for the first packet seems innocent enough; there is not much useful information, as you can see in Figure 9-10.

```
0000  00 d0 59 aa af 80 00 01  96 3c 3f a8 08 00 45 00   ..Y..... .<?...E.
0010  00 28 08 ed 40 00 7f 06  d9 ac 0a ea 00 ef 0a ea   .(..@... ........
0020  02 74 07 01 11 5c 76 be  16 50 cd 5a 82 b2 50 10   .t...\v. .P.Z..P.
0030  43 b2 59 73 00 00 00 00  00 00 00 00               C.Ys.... ....
Frame (frame), 60 bytes
```

Figure 9-10: No useful information can be discerned from packet 1.

Moving on to the second packet, however (Figure 9-11), we see a reference to the C:\WINNT\System32 directory. This is one of the most important directories on a Windows 2000 system, since it contains many of the system files used to load and run Windows. Seeing a network packet referencing this location is often a sign of trouble.

```
0000  00 80 ad d1 84 d7 00 d0  59 aa af 80 08 00 45 00   ........ Y.....E.
0010  00 3c 00 3a 40 00 80 06  e1 4b 0a ea 02 74 0a ea   .<.:@... .K...t..
0020  00 ef 11 5c 07 01 cd 5a  82 b2 76 be 16 50 50 18   ...\...Z ..v..PP.
0030  fb db 73 31 00 00 0d 0a  43 3a 5c 57 49 4e 4e 54   ..s1.... C:\WINNT
0040  5c 73 79 73 74 65 6d 33  32 3e                     \system3 2>
Data (data), 20 bytes
```

Figure 9-11: The reference to C:\WINNT\System32 means something might be accessing our system files.

Once again, the third packet provides no useful information, but the fourth shows something that may be cause for concern, as shown in Figure 9-12.

```
0000  00 d0 59 aa af 80 00 01  96 3c 3f a8 08 00 45 00   ..Y..... .<?...E.
0010  00 3a 08 ef 40 00 7f 06  d9 98 0a ea 00 ef 0a ea   .:..@... ........
0020  02 74 07 01 11 5c 76 be  16 50 cd 5a 82 c6 50 18   .t...\v. .P.Z..P.
0030  43 9e a0 4d 00 00 73 74  61 72 74 20 6d 73 62 6c   C..M..st art msbl
0040  61 73 74 2e 65 78 65 0a                            ast.exe.
Data (data), 18 bytes
```

Figure 9-12: Packet 4 shows a reference to msblast.exe.

The Packet Bytes pane of the fourth packet shows a direct reference to the file msblast.exe. If you were involved in IT during the latter part of 2003, this filename should jump out at you immediately. However, if you weren't, Google is your friend. A search for this name will bring up loads of information about the Blaster worm—the source of the problem on Eddy's computer.

Summary

In this scenario we were faced with a computer with virus-scanning software that was not functioning properly; the problem turned out to be the Blaster worm.

When you suspect that you may be dealing with a virus or worm, you can usually find out all you need to know about the threat by performing an Internet search for the symptoms. Once you identify the virus or worm you are dealing with, you can research it and learn how to fight it.

Covert Information

covertinfo.pcap In this scenario you're the network security officer at a large multinational corporation. You have just been alerted by your superior that an employee overheard two other employees discussing the possibility of sneaking off with some of the company's assets. Your task in this scenario is to monitor the computers of the two suspect employees to see if you can figure out their plans.

What We Know

This scenario is based on the speculation of another employee. While we can't yet verify if what was overheard is true or if it was just taken out of context, we do know that the two employees in question are very computer savvy, so our observations should be conducted with the utmost care.

Tapping into the Wire

Because we don't want our tech-savvy employees to know that we're onto them, we want to make absolutely sure that the computers we are monitoring show no signs of being watched. For this reason, we'll use port mirroring, even though we are within our own network. A separate mirror and capture will have to be set up for each computer being monitored.

Analysis

Throughout the course of these two employees' daily work, a lot of packets are generated. In most cases, these packets are legitimate, so the first step is to search for traffic that could be suspicious. Display filters make it easy to search for traffic such as DCEPRC, NetBIOS, or ICMP, which we should not see under normal circumstances. I've applied this filter to the covertinfo.pcap capture; the result is two packets from one employee's computer, as shown in Figure 9-13.

No. ▲	Time	Source	Destination	Protocol	Info
1	0.000000	10.100.17.48	10.100.18.5	ICMP	Echo (ping) request
2	0.000015	10.100.18.5	10.100.17.48	ICMP	Echo (ping) reply

Figure 9-13: ICMP? Why would these two employees be pinging each other?

These packets may look like standard ICMP packets, but the source and destination addresses belong to the computers of our two suspect employees. Why would they be pinging each other during the middle of the day?

Next, as with the previous scenario, we'll look at the Packet Bytes pane to see if we can find anything interesting in this ping packet. Upon doing so, we see something a bit alarming, as shown in Figure 9-14.

```
0000  00 15 c5 37 e1 c1 00 0b  db 71 d7 39 08 00 45 00   ...7.....  .q.9..E.
0010  00 a8 52 87 00 00 80 01  af d1 0a 64 11 30 0a 64   ..R.....  ...d.0.d
0020  12 05 08 00 1c 2f e4 0e  a3 0d bc 44 8d 15 00 00   ...../..  ...D....
0030  00 00 00 00 00 00 42 6c  75 65 43 68 61 74 31 30   ......Bl  ueChat10
0040  2e 31 30 30 2e 31 37 2e  34 38 20 20 20 54 72 61   .100.17.  48   Tra
0050  6e 73 66 65 72 20 61 6c  6c 20 6f 66 20 74 68 65   nsfer al  l of the
0060  20 66 75 6e 64 73 20 74  6f 20 61 63 63 6f 75 6e    funds t  o accoun
0070  74 20 6e 75 6d 62 65 72  20 31 31 39 32 38 32 38   t number   1192828
0080  32 33 31 2d 30 20 20 20  20 20 20 20 20 20 20 20   231-0
0090  20 20 20 20 20 20 20 20  20 20 20 20 20 20 20 20
00a0  20 20 20 20 20 20 20 20  20 20 20 20 20 20 20 20
00b0  20 20 20 20 20 20
```

Figure 9-14: This is definitely not a normal ping packet.

This ping packet is far from standard. As a matter of fact, it is carrying a secret payload that details more than our employees would care for us to know!

Summary

The technology used in this scenario is referred to as *Loki*; it is a means of sending information across the wire via hidden methods. The term *Loki* comes from the first project that ever embedded data into ICMP packets. In our situation, ICMP was used as the carrier to transmit messages between our two employees with malicious intent.

The use of covert channels of communication is not a new technology, but it is evolving constantly. It is not uncommon to find data hidden in other types of packets as well, such as TCP headers and ARP packets. Always remember the Packet Bytes pane—while you may not use it often, it's sometimes the only way to see the secrets a packet may contain.

A Hacker's Point of View

hackersview
.pcap

Throughout this book, we have looked at things from the point of view of a network administrator. But what happens when a hacker with some packet analysis knowledge decides to take a peek at what's on the wire? In this scenario we assume the identity of a hacker attempting to access sensitive information on his local company network.

What We Know

Even though you're an employee of the company you are trying to break into, you have limited access to network resources. The network is a run-of-the-mill Ethernet network, and it utilizes a few switches and routers. All of the computers on the network are running various versions of Windows with access privileges defined on a per-user basis.

Tapping into the Wire

Some hackers want to capture the passwords of network administrators to gain administrative access to a network. Others simply want to bring a network to its knees. In this case we want to access a router on the network and then do some serious damage. Network administrators are always tinkering with those things, so it should be simple enough to monitor the communication between a network admin and a router to intercept a password.

Luckily, both the network administrator and the target router are on the same subnet as the computer we will be coordinating our attack from. We'll use Cain & Abel to set up ARP cache poisoning between the network administrator's computer, 10.100.18.5, and the network router, 10.100.16.1, just as we did in Chapter 2.

Analysis

After a while, we manage to get a capture file that contains the telnet traffic of the network administrator logging into the router. For the sake of this scenario, Figure 9-15 shows only the traffic relating to this particular telnet session.

No. ·	Time	Source	Destination	Protocol	Info
1	0.000000	10.100.18.5	10.100.16.1	TCP	3756 > telnet [SYN] Seq=0 Len=0 MSS=1460
2	0.001244	10.100.16.1	10.100.18.5	TCP	telnet > 3756 [SYN, ACK] Seq=0 Ack=1 Win=8192 Len=0 MSS=1460
3	0.001263	10.100.18.5	10.100.16.1	TCP	3756 > telnet [ACK] Seq=1 Ack=1 Win=65535 Len=0
4	0.003143	10.100.16.1	10.100.18.5	TELNET	Telnet Data ...
5	0.003201	10.100.18.5	10.100.16.1	TELNET	Telnet Data ...
6	0.004161	10.100.16.1	10.100.18.5	TELNET	Telnet Data ...
7	0.150539	10.100.18.5	10.100.16.1	TCP	3756 > telnet [ACK] Seq=4 Ack=6 Win=65530 Len=0
8	0.151553	10.100.16.1	10.100.18.5	TELNET	Telnet Data ...
9	0.351722	10.100.18.5	10.100.16.1	TCP	3756 > telnet [ACK] Seq=4 Ack=16 Win=65520 Len=0
10	1.285806	10.100.18.5	10.100.16.1	TELNET	Telnet Data ...
11	1.287056	10.100.16.1	10.100.18.5	TCP	telnet > 3756 [ACK] Seq=16 Ack=5 Win=8192 Len=0
12	1.287275	10.100.16.1	10.100.18.5	TELNET	Telnet Data ...

Figure 9-15: It appears that we have found what we are looking for.

When we discussed telnet in Chapter 6, we noted that it typically uses cleartext in its transmission of data. Telnet is commonly used to remotely administer switches, servers, and routers, as it is here. Most of these devices have features that enable to you log in securely, usually via SSH, but this is something that system administrators often neglect. Since the communication is happening in the clear, we should be able to find the login credentials for this router with just a little patience.

Telnet is a sequential protocol, meaning that everything happens in a set series. Therefore, the best way to locate the login process is by stepping through the Telnet Data packets one by one. As we do, we see the beginning of the authentication process clearly in packet 8, as shown in Figure 9-16.

```
⊞ Frame 8 (64 bytes on wire, 64 bytes captured)
⊞ Ethernet II, Src: Enterasy_31:4a:f0 (00:11:88:31:4a:f0), Dst: Dell_37:e1:c1 (00:15:c5:37:e1:c1)
⊞ Internet Protocol, Src: 10.100.16.1 (10.100.16.1), Dst: 10.100.18.5 (10.100.18.5)
⊞ Transmission Control Protocol, Src Port: telnet (23), Dst Port: 3756 (3756), Seq: 6, Ack: 4, Len: 10
⊟ Telnet
    Data: Username:
```

Figure 9-16: To begin the authentication process, this packet requests a username.

If you look in the Packet Details pane in the Telnet field, you will see that the data being passed from the server is the request for a username. The next packet replying to the server should contain the username, but it's a bit trickier than that.

As you can see in Figure 9-17, packet 10 contains only the letter *a*. This doesn't sound like a typical username, and it isn't.

```
0000   00 11 88 31 4a f0 00 15   c5 37 e1 c1 08 00 45 00    ...1J... .7....E.
0010   00 29 50 9c 40 00 80 06   73 65 0a 64 12 05 0a 64    .)P.@... se.d...d
0020   10 01 0e ac 00 17 24 0f   27 9a e0 a9 10 7c 50 18    ......$. '....|P.
0030   ff f0 cc 7a 00 00 61                                 ...z..a
```

Figure 9-17: This packet contains the first piece of the puzzle, an a.

The next packet sent from the client to the server gives us another piece of the puzzle, the letter *d*, as shown in Figure 9-18. We're seeing the administrator's response to the server one packet at a time. This process continues for a few more packets until we can eventually spell out the word *admin*. Not too original, huh? It's probably the default.

```
0000   00 11 88 31 4a f0 00 15   c5 37 e1 c1 08 00 45 00    ...1J... .7....E.
0010   00 29 50 9f 40 00 80 06   73 62 0a 64 12 05 0a 64    .)P.@... sb.d...d
0020   10 01 0e ac 00 17 24 0f   27 9b e0 a9 10 7d 50 18    ......$. '....}P.
0030   ff ef c9 79 00 00 64                                 ...y..d
```

Figure 9-18: The pieces start coming together as we get more letters. Here we have a d.

At packet 24 we see a request for a password, as shown in Figure 9-19.

```
⊞ Frame 24 (64 bytes on wire, 64 bytes captured)
⊞ Ethernet II, Src: Enterasy_31:4a:f0 (00:11:88:31:4a:f0), Dst: Dell_37:e1:c1 (00:15:c5:37:e1:c1)
⊞ Internet Protocol, Src: 10.100.16.1 (10.100.16.1), Dst: 10.100.18.5 (10.100.18.5)
⊞ Transmission Control Protocol, Src Port: telnet (23), Dst Port: 3756 (3756), Seq: 23, Ack: 11, Len: 10
⊟ Telnet
     Data: Password:
```

Figure 9-19: The server requests a password from the network administrator.

Once again, we see packets going across the wire that give us the password one letter at a time (Figure 9-20).

```
0000   00 11 88 31 4a f0 00 15   c5 37 e1 c1 08 00 45 00    ...1J... .7....E.
0010   00 29 50 b2 40 00 80 06   73 4f 0a 64 12 05 0a 64    .)P.@... sO.d...d
0020   10 01 0e ac 00 17 24 0f   27 a1 e0 a9 10 8d 50 18    ......$. '.....P.
0030   ff df cb 73 00 00 62                                 ...s..b
```

Figure 9-20: The first letter of the password, b, makes its way across the wire.

We continue sniffing these packets until we have the complete password, *barrymanilow*. Not only did we manage to capture the router password, but we have also learned that the network administrator has excellent taste in music!

Summary

At this point, we have everything we need to bring down this network. Once inside the router's configuration, we can delete subnets, change ip helper-addresses, and do all sorts of other mischievous things that will cause the network administrator severe headaches.

The point of this scenario is not to show you how to anger your network guys, but rather to demonstrate the power someone with a little knowledge and a packet sniffer can have. With Wireshark and a few other simple tools, we have effectively found a way to completely terminate all function on this network.

10

SNIFFING INTO THIN AIR

The world of wireless networking is completely different from traditional (wired) networking. When considering wireless networking, we need to take into account issues like frequencies, standards, and unique security questions. Given these extra considerations, you can bet that the sniffing process changes completely.

This chapter is devoted to explaining the wireless sniffing process on both Windows- and Unix-based systems. As we discuss what makes wireless sniffing unique, we'll look at a few examples showing it in action.

Sniffing One Channel at a Time

The first thing to understand about sniffing wireless traffic is that you can only sniff one wireless channel at a time. Wireless networks in the United States can operate on one of eleven different channels (more are available internationally). Therefore, before you capture the traffic from a wireless client or access point, you must first identify the channel it is broadcasting on (Figure 10-1).

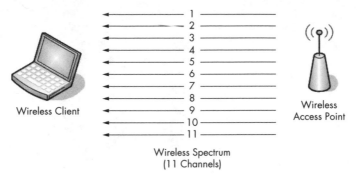

Wireless Client

Wireless Spectrum
(11 Channels)

Wireless
Access Point

Figure 10-1: Sniffing wirelessly can be tedious, since it can only be done one channel at a time.

The best way to find out which channel is being used is to channel hop. When you *channel hop*, you simply start a packet capture and switch rapidly from channel to channel until you see data that relates to what you are looking for. Although channel hopping isn't the most technical of solutions, it works.

Wireless Signal Interference

Unfortunately, sometimes we can't rely on the integrity of wireless communication. Because data is sent through the air, it's very likely that something will interfere with the signal. Wireless networks include features to handle interference, but they don't always work. Therefore, when capturing packets over a wireless network, pay close attention to your environment to ensure that there are no large sources of interference, such as large reflective surfaces, large rigid objects, microwaves, 2.4 GHz wireless phones, thick walls, and high-density surfaces.

Along these same lines, try to get as close as possible to the device you are analyzing. You can't hope to capture all of the packets sent by a device if you are one floor above it.

Wireless Card Modes

Before sniffing wireless packets, it is a good idea to familiarize yourself with the different modes in which a wireless card can operate.

Most users only use wireless cards in managed or ad-hoc modes, but other modes include master mode and monitor mode. I'll cover each mode below; a graphical representation of the way each one operates is shown in Figure 10-2.

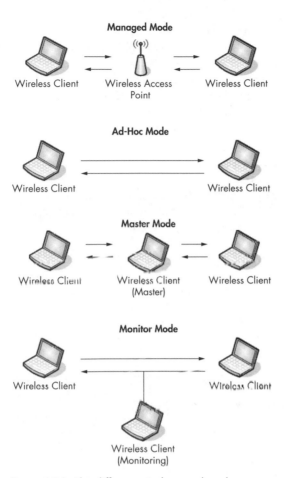

Figure 10-2: The different wireless card modes

Managed mode

Managed mode is used when your wireless client connects directly to a wireless access point (WAP). In these cases, the driver associated with the wireless NIC relies on the WAP to manage the entire communications process.

Ad-Hoc mode

Ad-hoc mode is used when you have a wireless network setup in which devices connect directly to each other. In this mode two wireless clients that want to communicate with each other share the responsibilities that a WAP would normally handle.

Master mode

Some higher-end wireless network cards also support master mode. *Master mode* allows the wireless NIC to work in conjunction with specialized driver software in order to allow the computer to act as a WAP for other devices.

Monitor mode

This is the most important mode for our purposes. *Monitor mode* is used when you want your wireless client to stop transmitting and receiving data and only listen to the packets flying through the air. In order for Wireshark to capture wireless packets, your wireless NIC and accompanying driver must support monitor mode. If you purchase a wireless network card for the purpose of analysis, be sure that it supports monitor mode (also known as RFMON mode).

Sniffing Wirelessly in Windows

Even if you have a wireless NIC that supports monitor mode, most Windows-based wireless NIC drivers won't allow you to change into this mode. You'll need a little extra hardware to get the job done.

Configuring AirPcap

AirPcap (from CACE Technologies, http://www.cacetech.com) is designed to overcome the limitations that Windows places on wireless packet analysis. *AirPcap* is a small USB device (Figure 10-3) resembling a Flash drive that is designed to capture wireless traffic. AirPcap uses the WinPcap driver discussed in Chapter 3 and a special client configuration utility.

Figure 10-3: The AirPcap device is very compact, making it easy to tote along with a laptop.

The AirPcap configuration program is simple to use; it has only a few configurable options. As shown in Figure 10-4, the AirPcap Control Panel gives you the following options:

Interface

You can select the device you are using for your capture here. Some advanced analysis scenarios may require you to use more than one AirPcap device to sniff simultaneously on multiple channels.

Blink Led

Clicking this button will make the LED lights on the AirPcap device blink. This is primarily used to identify the specific adapter you are using, if you are using multiple AirPcap devices.

Channel

In this field, you select the channel you want AirPcap to listen on.

Include 802.11 FCS in Frames

By default, some systems strip the last four checksum bits from wireless packets. This checksum, known as a *Frame Check Sequence (FCS)*, is used to ensure that packets have not been corrupted during transmission. Unless you have a specific reason to do otherwise, check this box to include the FCS checksums.

Capture Type

The two options here are 802.11 Only and 802.11 + Radio. The 802.11 Only option includes the standard 802.11 packet header on all capture packets. The 802.11 + Radio option includes this header and also prepends it with a *radiotap header*, which contains additional information about the packet, such as data rate, frequency, signal level, and noise level. Choose 802.11 + Radio in order to see all available packet information.

FCS Filter

Even if you uncheck the box next to the words *Include 802.11 FCS in Frames*, this option lets you filter out packets that FCS determines are corrupted. Use the Valid Frames option to only show those packets that FCS thinks can be received successfully.

WEP Configuration

This area (accessible on the Keys tab) allows you enter WEP decryption keys for the networks you will be sniffing. In order to be able to interpret data encrypted by WEP, you will have to enter the correct WEP keys into this field.

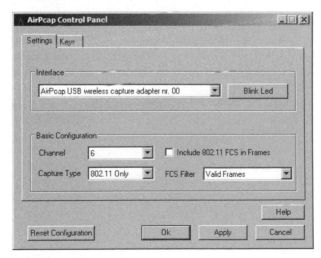

Figure 10-4: The AirPcap configuration program

Capturing Traffic with AirPcap

Once you have AirPcap installed and configured, the capture process should be familiar to you. Just follow these steps:

1. In Wireshark, select **Capture ▸ Options**.
2. Select your AirPcap device in the Interface selection box, as shown in Figure 10-5.

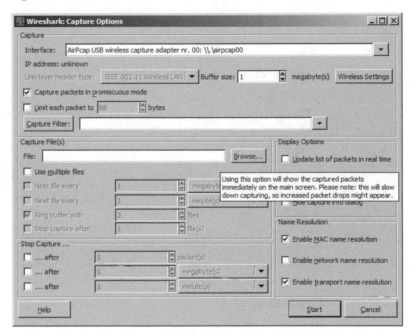

Figure 10-5: Choosing the AirPcap device as your capture interface

Everything on this screen should look familiar to you except for the Wireless Settings button. Clicking this button will give you the same options that the AirPcap utility gave you, as shown in Figure 10-6. Because Wireshark is completely integrated with AirPcap, anything configured in the client utility can also be configured from within Wireshark.

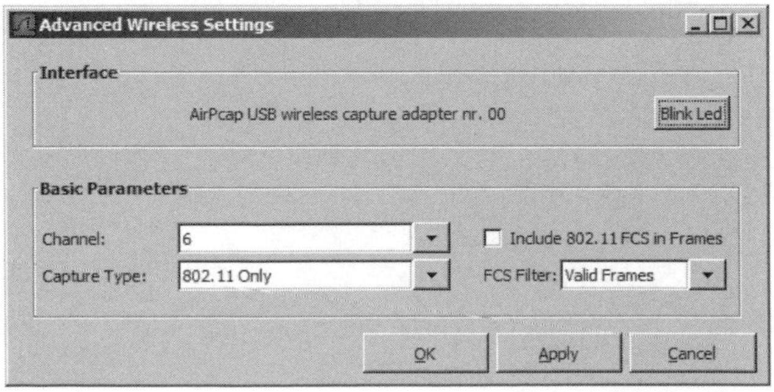

Figure 10-6: The Advanced Wireless Settings dialog allows you to configure AirPcap from within Wireshark.

3. Once you have everything configured to your liking, begin capturing packets by clicking the **Start** button.

Sniffing Wirelessly in Linux

Sniffing in Linux is simply a matter of enabling monitor mode on the wireless NIC and firing up Wireshark. Unfortunately, the procedure for enabling monitor mode differs with each model of wireless NIC, so I can't offer a definitive guide for it here. Your best bet is to do a quick Internet search for your NIC model for specific details.

One of the more common ways to enable monitor mode in Linux is through its built-in wireless extensions. You can access these wireless extensions with the iwconfig command. If you type iwconfig from the console, you should see results like this:

```
$ iwconfig
Eth0      no wireless extensions
Lo0       no wireless extensions
Eth1      IEEE 802.11g  ESSID:"Tesla Wireless Network"
          Mode:Managed Frequency:2.462 GHz Access Point: 00:02:2D:8B:70:2E
          Bit Rate: 54 Mb/s Tx-Power=20 dBm Sensitivity=8/0
          Retry Limit:7 RTS thr:off Fragment thr:off
          Power Management:off
          Link Quality=75/100 Signal level=-71 dBm Noise level=-86 dBm
          Rx invalid nwid:0 Rx invalid crypt:0 Rx invalid frag:0
          Tx excessive retries:0 Invalid misc:0 Missed beacon:2
```

The output from the iwconfig command shows that the Eth1 interface can be configured wirelessly. This is apparent because it shows data for the 802.11g protocol, whereas the interfaces Eth0 and Lo0 return the phrase no wireless extensions.

Along with all of the wireless information this command provides, such as the wireless card mode and frequency, notice that the second line under Eth1 shows that the mode is currently set to Managed. This is what we want to change.

In order to change the Eth1 interface to monitor mode, you must be logged in as the root user, either directly or via the switch user (su) command, shown here.

```
$ su
Password: <enter root password here>
```

Once you're root, you can type commands to configure the wireless interface options. To configure Eth1 to operate in monitor mode, type

```
# iwconfig eth1 mode monitor
```

Once in monitor mode, running the `iwconfig` command again should reflect your changes. Now ensure that the Eth1 interface is operational by typing

```
# iwconfig eth1 up
```

We'll also use the `iwconfig` command to perform the channel-hopping process discussed earlier in this chapter. Change the channel of the Eth1 interface by typing

```
# iwconfig eth1 channel 3
```

NOTE *You can do this on-the-fly as you are capturing packets, so don't hesitate to change channels at will. This command can also be scripted using various Linux scripting languages to make the process easier.*

Once you have completed these configurations, start Wireshark and begin your packet capture.

802.11 Packet Extras

80211traffic
.pcap

The main difference between the packet structure of a wireless packet and that of a standard packet is the addition of an 802.11 header. This header contains extra information about the packet and the medium used to transmit it, as shown in Figure 10-7.

```
⊞ Frame 1 (132 bytes on wire, 132 bytes captured)
⊟ IEEE 802.11
      Type/Subtype: Beacon frame (8)
  ⊞ Frame Control: 0x0080 (Normal)
      Duration: 0
      Destination address: Broadcast (ff:ff:ff:ff:ff:ff)
      Source address: D-Link_0b:22:ba (00:13:46:0b:22:ba)
      BSS Id: D-Link_0b:22:ba (00:13:46:0b:22:ba)
      Fragment number: 0
      Sequence number: 1352
⊞ IEEE 802.11 wireless LAN management frame
```

Figure 10-7: The 802.11 header contains extra wireless information about the packets.

To examine the packet shown in Figure 10-7 more closely, open the 80211traffic.pcap example file. Let's look at some of the interesting items in this header:

Type/Subtype   This specifies the type or subtype of the 802.11 packet shown. The type can be either management, data, or control.
Each type can also have a subtype. For example, the subtype of management packets can be beacon frame, authentication request, or disassociation notice.

Destination Address, Source Address, and BSS Id These fields contain the source, destination, and BSS Id addresses of the packet.

Fragment Number and Sequence Number These numbers are used to place the wireless packets in the appropriate order, similar to the way TCP assembles data streams.

802.11 Flags

The 802.11 header packet also contains a Flags section with even more wireless-specific information, as shown in Figure 10-8.

```
☐ Flags: 0x0
    DS status: Not leaving DS or network is operating in AD-HOC mode
    .... .0.. = More Fragments: This is the last fragment
    .... 0... = Retry: Frame is not being retransmitted
    ...0 .... = PWR MGT: STA will stay up
    ..0. .... = More Data: No data buffered
    .0.. .... = Protected flag: Data is not protected
    0... .... = Order flag: Not strictly ordered
```

Figure 10-8: The Flags section contains more wireless-specific packet information.

The Flags section includes these fields:

DS Status The *distribution status (DS) field* is used to determine which way the packet is traveling. If the From DS field is 1 and the To DS field is 0, then the packet is traveling from the WAP to the wireless client. If the values are the reverse, the packet is traveling from the wireless client to the WAP. If both numbers are 0, that usually means the packet is being broadcast from the WAP.

More Fragments This field is used when additional packets are required in order to read the packet being sent.

Retry The Retry option indicates whether or not the packet being transmitted is from the original transmission attempt (0) or a retransmission (1).

PWR MGT This field indicates whether or not a client is going into a power-saving state.

More Data This field is used by a WAP to inform a client that more packets are waiting to be sent to it.

Protected Flag This field is used to show whether or not a packet is using data encryption.

Order Flag The Order field is used to inform the recipient that the packet must be kept in a particular order, which prevents the recipient from reorganizing packets in order to increase throughput performance.

The Beacon Frame

The beacon frame is one of the most informative packets in a wireless transmission. A *beacon frame* is sent as a broadcast packet from a WAP across a wireless channel to notify any listening wireless clients that the WAP is available and to define the parameters that must be set in order to connect to it. Therefore, this type of broadcast packet contains a lot of useful information, as shown in Figure 10-9.

```
⊞ Frame 1 (132 bytes on wire, 132 bytes captured)
⊟ IEEE 802.11
     Type/Subtype: Beacon frame (8)
  ⊞ Frame Control: 0x0080 (Normal)
     Duration: 0
     Destination address: Broadcast (ff:ff:ff:ff:ff:ff)
     Source address: D-Link_0b:22:ba (00:13:46:0b:22:ba)
     BSS Id: D-Link_0b:22:ba (00:13:46:0b:22:ba)
     Fragment number: 0
     Sequence number: 1352
⊞ IEEE 802.11 wireless LAN management frame
```

Figure 10-9: This beacon frame tells you everything you could ever want to know about the WAP.

Some of the information that you might see in a beacon frame includes the following:

SSID parameter set   This is the SSID that the WAP is broadcasting.

Supported rates   This lists the supported rates of data throughput provided by the WAP and specifies whether the protocol used is 802.11b or 802.11g.

DS parameter set   This shows the channel the WAP is broadcasting on.

Extended supported rates   This shows other supported throughput rates provided by the WAP.

Vendor-specific information   This section shows vendor-specific information about the WAP, including the chipset manufacturer, tag number, and tag length. (Note that the chipset manufacturer is not always the same as the WAP manufacturer.)

Wireless-Specific Columns

Wireshark typically shows six individual columns in the Packet List pane, all of which should look familiar to you. However, due to the added overhead when analyzing and interpreting wireless packets, Wireshark displays two more very useful columns: RSSI and TX Rate. The *Received Signal Strength Indication (RSSI)* column shows the radio frequency (RF) signal strength of a captured packet, while the *TX Rate* column shows the data rate of a captured packet, as shown in Figure 10-10. Both indicators can be of great help when you are troubleshooting wireless connections. In fact, even if your wireless client software says you have excellent signal strength, doing a capture with these columns enabled can show you a number that may or may not support that claim.

Figure 10-10: These two additional columns make a big difference in how you look at things during analysis.

To add these columns to the Packet List pane, follow these steps:

1. Choose **Edit ▸ Preferences**.

2. Navigate to the **Columns** section and click **New**.

3. Type RSSI in the Title field, and select **IEEE 802.11 RSSI** in the Format drop-down box.

4. Repeat this process again for the TX Rate column, titling it appropriately and selecting **IEEE 802.11 TX Rate** in the Format section. Figure 10-11 shows what this window should look like after you have added information for both columns.

5. Click **OK** in the Preferences dialog to save your changes.

6. Restart Wireshark to display the new columns.

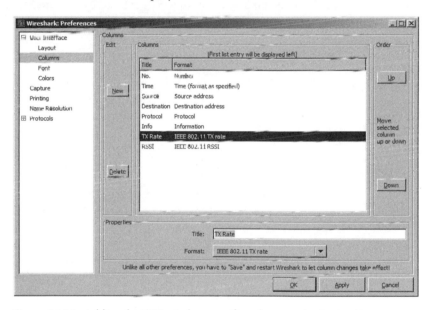

Figure 10-11: Adding the IEEE wireless-specific columns to the Packet List pane

Wireless-Specific Filters

We discussed the benefits of capture filters in Chapter 4. In a wired infrastructure it is a lot easier to filter the traffic you want to capture, since each device has its own dedicated cable. In a wireless network, however, all traffic generated by wireless clients coexists on shared channels, which means that a capture of any one channel may contain traffic from dozens of clients. This section is devoted to some packet filters that can be used to help you find the traffic you want.

Filtering Traffic for a Specific BSS Id

Each WAP in a network has a unique identifying name called its *Basic Service Set Identifier (BSS Id)*. This name is sent in every wireless management and data frame the access point transmits. (See "802.11 Packet Extras" on page 142.)

Once you know the name of the BSS Id you want to examine, all you really have to do is to find a packet that has been sent from that particular WAP. Wireshark shows the transmitting WAP in the Info column of the Packet List pane, so finding this information is typically pretty easy.

Once you have a packet from the particular WAP you want, find its BSS Id field in the 802.11 header, as shown in Figure 10-9. This is the address you will base your filter on.

After you have found the BSS Id MAC address (listed in the Packet Details pane) you can use the filter `wlan.bssid.eq 00:11:23:44:55:66` to show only the traffic flowing through that particular WAP.

Filtering Specific Wireless Packet Types

Earlier in this chapter, we discussed the different types of wireless packets you can see on a network. You will often need to be able to filter based upon these types and subtypes. Use Table 10-1 as a reference to help you to build the filters you need.

Filtering Specific Data Types

Although wireless management packets are very important for some types of analysis, our analysis may only require looking at the data being passed through the air—for instance, if we need to track down rogue wireless clients or identify the possibility of unwanted information disclosure over the wireless network. Therefore, we need to know how to filter only data packets.

To filter out all but the data packets in a capture file, use the capture filter `wlan.fc.type eq 2`. (If you reference Table 10-1, you will see that a frame type of 2 will show us all data pertaining to the data frames.)

The only downside to using this filter is that it still allows for the display of NULL data packets. These packets are used by certain WAPs and wireless NICs to alert the network that they are about to switch channels. If you don't need to see these NULL packets, filter them out by expanding the filter we created earlier and removing the NULL packet subtype. The filter looks like this when completed:

```
(wlan.fc.type eq 2) and !(wlan.fc.subtype eq4).
```

Differentiating between unencrypted and encrypted data is a great way to identify rogue WAPs on a network or to determine whether sensitive information is being sent in cleartext.

Table 10-1: Wireless Types/Subtypes and Associated Filter Syntax

Frame Type/Subtype	Filter Syntax
Management frames	wlan.fc.type eq 0
Control frames	wlan.fc.type eq 1
Data frames	wlan.fc.type eq 2
Association request	wlan.fc.type_subtype eq 0
Association response	wlan.fc.type_subtype eq 1
Reassociation request	wlan.fc.type_subtype eq 2
Reassociation response	wlan.fc.type_subtype eq 3
Probe request	wlan.fc.type_subtype eq 4
Probe response	wlan.fc.type_subtype eq 5
Beacon	wlan.fc.type_subtype eq 8
Disassociate	wlan.fc.type_subtype eq 10
Authentication	wlan.fc.type_subtype eq 11
Deauthentication	wlan.fc.type_subtype eq 12
Action frames	wlan.fc.type_subtype eq 13
Block ACK requests	wlan.fc.type_subtype eq 24
Block ACK	wlan.fc.type_subtype eq 25
Power save poll	wlan.fc.type_subtype eq 26
Request to send	wlan.fc.type_subtype eq 27
Clear to send	wlan.fc.type_subtype eq 28
ACK	wlan.fc.type_subtype eq 29
Contention free period end	wlan.fc.type_subtype eq 30
NULL data	wlan.fc.type_subtype eq 36
QoS data	wlan.fc.type_subtype eq 40
Null QoS data	wlan.fc.type_subtype eq 44

Recall the Protected flag from the section "802.11 Flags" on page 143; it is the flag used to identify a packet as being encrypted or unencrypted. We'll base our filter on this flag.

Recall that the Protected flag bit is set to 0 when no encryption is being used and it is set to 1 if the packet is encrypted with a protocol such as WEP, WPA, TKIP, and so on. Therefore, using a filter of

```
wlan.fc.protected eq 0
```

will show us all packets that are not encrypted. By the same token, a filter of

```
wlan.fc.protected eq 1
```

will show only encrypted traffic.

There are hundreds of ways to filter your captured wireless traffic. You can view many of these wireless capture filters on the Wireshark wiki at http://wiki.wireshark.org.

A Bad Connection Attempt

Now let's take a look at a specific scenario related to wireless packet analysis. In this scenario, Justin is trying to configure his laptop to access the wireless network at his office. Unfortunately, it just isn't working.

What We Know

The network Justin is trying to connect to uses the shared authentication method with WEP encryption on channel one. Justin should simply be able to enter these settings into his wireless client to connect, but when he does, the connection fails.

Tapping into the ~~Wire~~ Air

In this situation, capturing packets from the air requires the same thought process as capturing packets on a wired connection. Because the process seems to fail when Justin tries to connect to the wireless network, we'll capture packets at that time. The best way to do this is by using the AirPcap device, set to channel one.

Analysis

Since we have yet to look at any wireless captures, we don't know what a successful wireless authentication and association sequence looks like. Let's look at a capture file of this process when it's working correctly—open the example file SuccessfulWEPAuth.pcap, which shows a successful sequence on Justin's network.

The wireless on Justin's network is set up using WEP shared-key security. A *Wired Equivalent Privacy (WEP) key* is a hexadecimal or alphanumeric code that serves as a type of password used to encrypt the communication between a WAP and a wireless client (i.e., the user attempting to connect to the wireless network). In order to connect to a WAP, the wireless client must first complete a challenge and response with the WAP in order to verify that the correct WEP key is being used. This challenge and response begins in packet 4 of the capture file, as shown in Figure 10-12.

```
⊟ Challenge text
     Tag Number: 16 (Challenge text)
     Tag length: 128
     Tag interpretation: Challenge text: D4ABB116F5B6C6CF1EC74B95A5389E7D341CC3D87A2F9F95...
```

Figure 10-12: The WAP issues challenge text to the wireless client.

The WAP responds to the connection attempt by sending a challenge statement to the client. This statement is an encrypted string of text that must be decrypted by the client (with the appropriate WEP key) and then sent back to the WAP, as shown in Figure 10-13.

```
⊟ WEP parameters
    Initialization Vector: 0x0cf79e
    Key Index: 0
    WEP ICV: 0x409d2512 (not verified)
  Data (147 bytes)
```

Figure 10-13: The wireless client sends the
unencrypted challenge text back to the WAP.

In packet 6 the wireless client sends back the unencrypted challenge text, and the WAP to replies with a message stating that the authentication process was successful, as shown in Figure 10-14.

```
⊟ Fixed parameters (6 bytes)
    Authentication Algorithm: Shared key (1)
    Authentication SEQ: 0x0004
    Status code: Successful (0x0000)
```

Figure 10-14: The WAP alerts the client that
authentication was successful.

Finally, after a successful authentication, the client can transmit an association request, receive an acknowledgment, and connect, as shown in Figure 10-15.

No. ▴	Time	Source	Destination	Protocol	Info
10	0.145465	GemtekTe_30:b0:af	Enterasy_6b:68:30	IEEE 8	Association Request,SN-44,FN=0, SSID: "DENVEROFFICE"
11	0.145839		GemtekTe_30:b0:af	IEEE 8	Acknowledgement
12	0.148466	Enterasy_6b:67:28	Broadcast	IEEE 8	Data,SN=1390,FN=0
13	0.149090	Enterasy_6b:68:30	GemtekTe_30:b0:af	IEEE 8	Association Response,SN=1391,FN=0
14	0.149464		Enterasy_6b:68:30	IEEE 8	Acknowledgement

Figure 10-15: The authentication process is followed by a sweet and simple association request and response.

Now that we know what a connection to a WAP should look like, let's look at the capture file from Justin's connection attempt. As we see in packet 3 (shown in Figure 10-16), the WAP sends challenge text to Justin's computer, so we know that the two devices can see each other.

```
⊟ IEEE 802.11 wireless LAN management frame
  ⊟ Fixed parameters (6 bytes)
      Authentication Algorithm: Shared key (1)
      Authentication SEQ: 0x0002
      Status code: Successful (0x0000)
  ⊟ Tagged parameters (130 bytes)
    ⊟ Challenge text
        Tag Number: 16 (challenge text)
        Tag length: 128
        Tag interpretation: challenge text: DEFC7D3DDCBC57CC85FFCE1687FAC6E5528E4DD0619BF5B1...
```

Figure 10-16: The WAP sends challenge text to Justin's computer.

Packet 5 (in Figure 10-17) shows the wireless client sending its response to the server, which tells us that these devices are attempting to communicate.

```
     Destination address: Enterasy_6b:68:30 (00:11:88:6b:68:30)
     Source address: GemtekTe_30:b0:af (00:14:a5:30:b0:af)
     BSS Id: Enterasy_6b:68:30 (00:11:88:6b:68:30)
     Fragment number: 0
     Sequence number: 43
 ⊟ WEP parameters
     Initialization Vector: 0x26709d
     Key Index: 0
     WEP ICV: 0xc800a5b7 (not verified)
 Data (147 bytes)
```

Figure 10-17: Justin's computer sends its response to the challenge text back to the WAP.

At this point in the progression, we should now see a response from the WAP confirming that the authentication process was successful. But instead, we see something else, as shown in Figure 10-18. The authentication fails.

```
⊟ IEEE 802.11 wireless LAN management frame
  ⊟ Fixed parameters (6 bytes)
      Authentication Algorithm: Unknown (58901)
      Authentication SEQ: 0x884c
      Status code: Received an Authentication frame with authentication sequence transaction sequence number out of expected sequence
```

Figure 10-18: Apparently, the authentication wasn't successful.

The message sent from the WAP to Justin's computer tells us exactly what is going on: The sequence numbers are out of order. This means that the response Justin's computer gave to the challenge text was not correct—therefore, the WEP key used to decrypt the challenge text has either not been entered or has been entered incorrectly.

Summary

The sad truth about troubleshooting wireless network problems is that wireless client software usually doesn't report specific problems: The client either connects or it doesn't. Luckily, wireless packet analysis techniques allow us to see exactly what is going on and to more efficiently troubleshoot wireless networks.

Final Thoughts

Wireless networks are becoming a staple in the corporate environment. As focus shifts to wireless, we must be able to troubleshoot both wired and wireless networks. The skills and concepts taught in this chapter should help you to understand the intricacies of troubleshooting a wireless network with packet analysis.

11

FURTHER READING

Although Wireshark is the only tool required for packet analysis in most cases, several other tools and websites may come in handy when you're performing packet analysis.

Cain & Abel (http://www.oxid.it)

You may remember Cain & Abel from our discussion of ARP cache poisoning in Chapter 2. Along with being able to perform ARP cache poisoning, Cain & Abel also has several other great features including password sniffing and recovery, VoIP recording, and general network information gathering capabilities.

PingPlotter

This program is an extension of the ICMP ping utility and allows you take the text output you would normally get from a ping and graph it so that you can better analyze trends in network connectivity. This capability comes in handy when you want to do long-term analysis. You can download PingPlotter from http://www.pingplotter.com/download.html.

Superscan 4

Superscan 4 is a simple network scanning utility. The main draw is its incredible scanning speed; Superscan scans efficiently and quickly when you are in a hurry to get the information you need. You'll find a lot of use for this tool when collecting information about a host or network. You can download Superscan from http://www.foundstone.com/resources/proddesc/superscan.htm.

RUMINT

RUMINT(pronounced *room-int*) is a freely distributed application that you can use to visualize captured packet data. It provides several detailed graph and visualization options to help you better understand and model the packets you have captured. You can read more about RUMINT at http://www.rumint.org.

Engage Packet Builder (http://www.engagesecurity.com/products/engagepacketbuilder)

The Engage Packet Builder by Engage Security (shown in Figure 11-1) allows you to construct and transmit your own customized packets. You might use these packets simply for educational purposes or to test firewalls, intrusion detection systems, or devices susceptible to flooding attacks.

You can use Engage Packet Builder to craft individual packets with numerous options, and you can use scripts to automate certain aspects of packet creation.

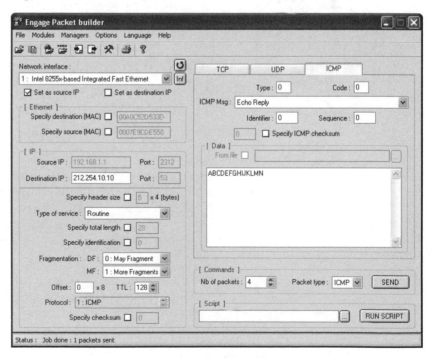

Figure 11-1: Engage Security's Engage Packet Builder

IANA (http://www.iana.org)

The Internet Assigned Number Authority (IANA) oversees the allocation of IP addresses and protocol number assignments for North America. Its website offers some valuable reference tools, such as the ability to look up port numbers, view information related to top-level domain names, and browse companion sites to find and view RFCs.

Wireshark Wiki and Mailing List (http://www.wireshark.org)

Since Wireshark is a community-driven project, the Wireshark wiki and mailing list are Wireshark's primary means of support.

Wireshark University (http://www.wiresharktraining.com)

Wireshark University was launched in March 2007 by several key players in the Wireshark and packet analysis community, including Gerald Combs (author of Wireshark), Laura Chappell (Senior Protocol Analyst of the Packet Analysis Institute), John Bruno (co-founder of CACE technologies), and Loris Degioanni (author of WinPcap).

Wireshark University is the premier Wireshark training resource. In addition to its self-paced video training offerings, it also offers a Wireshark certification program.

AFTERWORD

I hope that you have managed to get everything out of this book that I have put into it. Packet analysis is both a science and an art, similar to medicine—the network is the patient and you are the physician. Just as a doctor knows the human anatomy and the science behind medicine, a network administrator knows the elements of network architecture and the protocols behind a network. Still, regardless of how much of the science you understand behind something, you can't be the best until you truly understand how it works and have some experience behind you. This is why seasoned doctors are the go-to people when it comes to complex cases. The same applies for network administrators.

The main goal of this book has been to introduce you to the tools and concepts that you must master in order to learn how to get a feel for a network. The more you use packet analysis and the more real-world experience you gain, the more effectively you will be able to solve even the most complex network problems. I challenge you to use Wireshark to go out and explore your own network and others (with permission, of course) and examine communication at the packet level. It is only there that you will really learn what it means to delve into a network and see exactly what is happening on the wire. This is the essence of practical packet analysis.

INDEX

D

data
analysis, by packet sniffer, 3
compression, 4
encapsulation, 7
encryption, 4
WEP key for, 148
packets, filtering wireless traffic
for, 146–148
Data Link layer (OSI model), 6
DCEPRC packets, 96
DEB-based distributions, installing
Wireshark on, 31
Debian system, installing
Wireshark on, 31
Decode As dialog, 54
default gateway, 84–86
Degioanni, Loris, 153
Department of Defense (DoD) model
vs. OSI model, 5
Destination unreachable messages,
79–80, 95
destunreachable.pcap file, 79
DHCP (Dynamic Host Configuration
Protocol), 62–63
Discover packet, 63
Offer packet, 63
dhcp.pcap file, 62
dialog, 5
dictionary attack, 126
Discover packet (DHCP), 63
Display Filter dialog, 49–50
display filters, 46
using Filter Expression dialog
to create, 47
for finding packets, 40
for FTP login attempts, 126
sample expressions, 49
saving, 49–50
DNS (Domain Name System), 68–69
dns.pcap file, 68
documentation, online, for
Wireshark, 28
DoD (Department of Defense) model
vs. OSI model, 5
domain name resolution, and packets
in capture file, 53
Domain Name System (DNS), 68–69

double-vision.pcap file, 107
downloading data, HTTP packets
indicating, 87
DS Status field in 802.11 packet
header, 143
Duplicate ACK packets, 102
Dynamic Host Configuration Protocol
(DHCP), 62–63

E

Echo (ping) reply packets, 79, 105
edge router, using to analyze slow
network problems, 111–113
Edit menu
▸ Find Packet, 40
▸ Preferences, 34
▸ Set Time Reference, 44
editing color filters, 37
email
attachments, 115
server, slow network for, 114–115
email-troubles.pcap file, 114
encapsulation of data, 7–8
encryption of data, 4
WEP key for, 148
endpoints, viewing, 57–58
Engage Packet Builder, 152
Enterasys, port mirroring command
for, 19
errors
correcting, 4
detecting, 4
viewing in Expert Infos window, 101
Ethereal, 27
Ethernet, and packet size limitations, 81
evilprogram.pcap file, 92
Expert Infos window, 100–101
exporting capture files, 42

F

FCS (Frame Check Sequence), 139
file format, for capture file, 41
File menu
▸ Export, 42
▸ Merge, 42
▸ Print, 43
▸ Save As, 41

Electronic Frontier Foundation
Defending Freedom in the Digital World

Free Speech. Privacy. Innovation. Fair Use. Reverse Engineering. If you care about these rights in the digital world, then you should join the Electronic Frontier Foundation (EFF). EFF was founded in 1990 to protect the rights of users and developers of technology. EFF is the first to identify threats to basic rights online and to advocate on behalf of free expression in the digital age.

The Electronic Frontier Foundation Defends Your Rights!
Become a Member Today!
http://www.eff.org/support/

Current EFF projects include:

Protecting your fundamental right to vote. Widely publicized security flaws in computerized voting machines show that, though filled with potential, this technology is far from perfect. EFF is defending the open discussion of e-voting problems and is coordinating a national litigation strategy addressing issues arising from use of poorly developed and tested computerized voting machines.

Ensuring that you are not traceable through your things. Libraries, schools, the government and private sector businesses are adopting radio frequency identification tags, or RFIDs – a technology capable of pinpointing the physical location of whatever item the tags are embedded in. While this may seem like a convenient way to track items, it's also a convenient way to do something less benign: track people and their activities through their belongings. EFF is working to ensure that embrace of this technology does not erode your right to privacy.

Stopping the FBI from creating surveillance backdoors on the Internet. EFF is part of a coalition opposing the FBI's expansion of the Communications Assistance for Law Enforcement Act (CALEA), which would require that the wiretap capabilities built into the phone system be extended to the Internet, forcing ISPs to build backdoors for law enforcement.

Providing you with a means by which you can contact key decision-makers on cyber-liberties issues. EFF maintains an action center that provides alerts on technology, civil liberties issues and pending legislation to more than 50,000 subscribers. EFF also generates a weekly online newsletter, EFFector, and a blog that provides up-to-the minute information and commentary.

Defending your right to listen to and copy digital music and movies. The entertainment industry has been overzealous in trying to protect its copyrights, often decimating fair use rights in the process. EFF is standing up to the movie and music industries on several fronts.

Check out all of the things we're working on at http://www.eff.org and join today or make a donation to support the fight to defend freedom online.

ELECTRONIC FRONTIER FOUNDATION · 454 SHOTWELL STREET · SAN FRANCISCO, CA 94110 · 415.436.9333

Introducing Wireshark University

Instructor-led and self-paced courses focused on Wireshark functionality, TCP/IP Analysis, network troubleshooting and network forensics.

Wireshark University (WSU) was founded by **Laura Chappell**, renowned industry protocol analyst of the Protocol Analysis Institute, in cooperation with **Gerald Combs**, original author of Wireshark, and WinPcap creator **Loris Degioanni**, both of CACE Technologies.

The Wireshark Certified Network Analyst (WCNA) certification program validates a candidate's ability to use Wireshark to perform network troubleshooting and forensics.

Wireshark University Course List

WSU01: Wireshark Functionality and Fundamentals

Learn how to use Wireshark efficiently and effectively by placing Wireshark in the ideal location to capture traffic (even on a switched network). Learn to focus on key traffic using filters and display your results with Wireshark's graphs.

WSU02: TCP/IP Network Analysis

This course focuses on both normal and abnormal communications of the TCP/IP suite and common applications such as DHCP, DNS, FTP, Telnet, HTTP, POP, and SMTP.

WSU03: Troubleshooting Network Performance

This course focuses on the causes of poor network performance, including packet-loss, retransmissions, high latency, low throughput rates, minimal bandwidth, application errors, configuration faults, resolution problems, and protocol behavior problems.

WSU04: Network Forensics and Security

This course focuses on network forensics, including capture locations, stealth-mode capture, optimal capture and display filters, validating encrypted logins, identifying reconnaissance processes, locating header and payload signatures, and catching penetration tests, malware behavior, backdoor communications, and virus traffic.

For course information, schedules, and pricing, visit www.wiresharkU.com.

About Wireshark Certification

The Wireshark Certified Network Analyst (WCNA) program consists of a single online test based on the content and focus of the following Wireshark courses:

- WSU01: Wireshark Functionality and Fundamentals
- WSU02: TCP/IP Network Analysis
- WSU03: Troubleshooting Network Performance
- WSU04: Network Forensics and Security

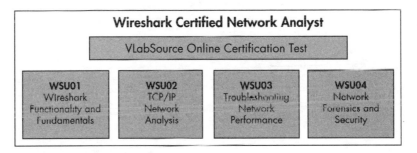

The WSU Certification Test is a hands-on test administered in a virtual environment. The candidate is provided access to a virtual host running Wireshark on a network that is experiencing various performance- and security-related problems.

The Wireshark University FIN Bit Magazine

Register online to receive notification of each release date for the FIN Bit Magazine, Wireshark University's free quarterly magazine filled with Wireshark tips and tricks, developer notes, trace files, and more.

Questions? Contact us at info@wiresharkU.com.

LINUX FIREWALLS
Attack Detection and Response with iptables, psad, and fwsnort

by MICHAEL RASH

Linux firewalls provide capabilities that rival commercial firewalls and are built upon the powerful Netfilter infrastructure in the Linux kernel. *Linux Firewalls: Attack Detection and Response with iptables, psad, and fwsnort* explores using iptables as an intrusion detection system (IDS) by combining it with Snort rulesets and custom open-source software created by the author. Providing concrete examples to illustrate concepts, the book discusses Linux firewall log analysis and policies, passive network authentication and authorization, exploit packet traces, Snort ruleset emulation, and more. Perl and C code snippets are included to help readers maximize the deployment of Linux firewalls as effective mechanisms for the detection and prevention of various network-based attacks.

JULY 2007, 304 PP., $49.95
ISBN 978-1-59327-141-1

PGP & GPG
Email for the Practical Paranoid

by MICHAEL W. LUCAS

Governments worldwide, major manufacturers, medical facilities, and many of the smartest computer experts around trust their secure communications to PGP (Pretty Good Privacy). But, while PGP works amazingly when all is in order, it isn't always easy to configure and can be very tricky to troubleshoot. And email security is hardly the sort of thing you want to leave to chance. *PGP & GPG: Email for the Practical Paranoid* is for moderately skilled geeks who are unfamiliar with public-key cryptography but who want to protect their communication on the cheap. Author Michael W. Lucas offers this easy-to-read, informal tutorial on PGP, so you can dive in right away.

APRIL 2006, 216 PP., $24.95
ISBN 978-1-59327-071-2

THE TCP/IP GUIDE
A Comprehensive, Illustrated Internet Protocols Reference

by CHARLES M. KOZIEROK

Finally, here's an encyclopedic, comprehensible, well-illustrated, and completely current guide to the TCP/IP protocol suite for both newcomers and seasoned professionals. This complete reference details the core protocols that make TCP/IP internetworks function, as well as the most important TCP/IP applications. It includes full coverage of PPP, ARP, IP, IPv6, IP NAT, IPSec, Mobile IP, ICMP, and much more. It also offers an in-depth view of the TCP/IP protocol suite, and it describes networking fundamentals and the important OSI Reference Model.

OCTOBER 2005, 1616 PP., $79.95 HARDCOVER
ISBN 978-159327-047-6

SILENCE ON THE WIRE

A Field Guide to Passive Reconnaissance and Indirect Attacks

by MICHAL ZALEWSKI

Author Michal Zalewski has long been known and respected in the hacking and security communities for his intelligence, curiosity, and creativity, and this book is truly unlike anything else out there. In *Silence on the Wire: A Field Guide to Passive Reconnaissance and Indirect Attacks*, Zalewski shares his expertise and experience to explain how computers and networks work, how information is processed and delivered, and what security threats lurk in the shadows. No humdrum technical white paper or how-to manual for protecting one's network, this book is a fascinating narrative that explores a variety of unique and often quite elegant security challenges that defy classification and eschew the traditional attacker-victim model.

APRIL 2005, 312 PP., $39.95
ISBN 978-1-59327-046-9

NAGIOS

System and Network Monitoring

by WOLFGANG BARTH

This book shows readers how to configure and use Nagios, an open-source system- and network-monitoring tool. Nagios makes it possible to continuously monitor network services (SMTP, POP3, HTTP, NNTP, PING, and so on), host resources (processor load, disk and memory usage, running processes, log files, and so on), and environmental factors (such as temperature). When Nagios detects a problem, it communicates the information to the sys admin via email, pager, SMS, or other user-defined method; current status information, historical logs, and reports can also be accessed via a web browser. *Nagios: System and Network Monitoring* covers the Nagios core as well as all standard Nagios plug-ins and selected third-party plug-ins, and it shows readers how to write their own plug-ins. The book covers Nagios 2.0 and is backward compatible with earlier versions. It has been co-published with Open Source Press.

MAY 2006, 464 PP. $44.95
ISBN 978-1-59327-070-4

PHONE:
800.420.7240 OR
415.863.9900
MONDAY THROUGH FRIDAY,
9 A.M. TO 5 P.M. (PST)

FAX:
415.863.9950
24 HOURS A DAY,
7 DAYS A WEEK

EMAIL:
SALES@NOSTARCH.COM

WEB:
WWW.NOSTARCH.COM

MAIL:
NO STARCH PRESS
555 DE HARO ST, SUITE 250
SAN FRANCISCO, CA 94107
USA

COLOPHON

Practical Packet Analysis was laid out in Adobe FrameMaker. The font families used are New Baskerville for body text, Futura for headings and tables, and Dogma for titles.

The book was printed and bound at Malloy Incorporated in Ann Arbor, Michigan. The paper is Glatfelter Thor 60# Antique, which is made from 15 percent postconsumer content. The book uses a RepKover binding, which allows it to lay flat when open.

UPDATES

Visit **http://www.nostarch.com/packet.htm** for updates, errata, and other information. All of the capture files used in this book are available at **http://www.nostarch.com/packet.htm** and **http://www.chrissanders.org/PPA**.